"We Are Your Servants"

Augustine's Homilies on Ministry

Introduction by

Cardinal Michael Pellegrino

translated by

Audrey Fellowes

edited by

John E. Rotelle, O.S.A.

Augustinian Press
1986

Nihil Obstat: James McGrath
        Censor Librorum
Imprimatur: John Cardinal Krol
        Archbishop of Philadelphia

This book was originally published in Italian (*Il Pastore d'Anime*) by Edizioni Esperienze in 1960.

© 1986 by Brothers of the Order of Hermits of Saint Augustine, Inc. All rights reserved.

Library of Congress Card Catalog Number   86-71645

Augustinian Press
P.O. Box 338
Villanova, PA 19085

Set in Palatino and Zapf Chancery by Exordium. Printed in the United States.

In loving memory
of
Howard and Jeanne Brass

An everlasting tribute.

On the occasion
of
the 1600th Anniversary
of the
Conversion of Saint Augustine of Hippo
386/387 - 1986/1987
we present this book in English translation,
the sermons of Augustine on ministry,
to the
bishops of the Catholic Church,
in particular
Pope John Paul II
and
all the bishops of the English-speaking world.
May these words of Augustine
encourage, inspire, and console them
in their ministry to the People of God.

The Augustinians

Contents

Foreword	ix
Introduction The Priesthood as Service in Saint Augustine's Thought	1
Chapter 1 The Good Shepherd (Homilies on John's Gospel, 46)	15
Chapter 2 The Bishop's Mission and Duties (Sermon 340A or Sermon Guelferbytanus 32)	29
Chapter 3 Ordination Anniversary (Sermon 340)	49
Chapter 4 The Shepherd's Cares (Sermon 339)	55
Chapter 5 The Harvest (Sermon 101)	79
Chapter 6 Love and Sacrifice (Homilies on John's Gospel, 123, 4-5)	95
Chapter 7 God Warns the Shepherds (Sermon 46, 1-11)	105
Chapter 8 The Bishop's Collaborators (Sermon 94)	121

Chapter 9
Shepherds and Hirelings (Sermon 137) 125

Chapter 10
Unity Through Love (Sermon 138) 149

Illustrations

p. x. — Saint Augustine the Writer by B. Gozzoli (1465), Church of Saint Augustine, San Gimignano, Italy.

p. 15 — Saint Augustine preaching, teaching, and baptizing, detail of the tomb of Saint Augustine, Pavia, Italy.

p. 29 — Augustine washes the feet of the pilgrim Christ by Esteban Murillo (1618-1682).

p.49 — The Consecration of Augustine as Bishop by Martin Pepijn (1626).

p. 55 — Saint Augustine at prayer by Jean Leclerc (1585).

p. 79 — Augustine listens to the preaching of Ambrose by M. Gunther (1742), Rottenbuch.

p. 95 — Augustine, at the end of his life, heals a sick person (Bolswert Engravings, 1624).

p. 105 — Augustine defends truth from the altarpiece by Jaime Huguet (1463), Museum of Catalan Art, Barcelona, Spain.

p. 121 — Augustine encounters the child Jesus on the beach by Esteban Murillo (1618-1682).

p. 125 — Augustine presides at the Council of Carthage (Bolswert Engravings, 1624).

p. 149 — Augustine washes the feet of the pilgrim Christ, Holy Savior Cathedral, Bruges, Belgium.

p. 156 — Tomb of Saint Augustine, Pavia, Italy.

Foreword

It has always been my desire to publish this collection of Saint Augustine's Homilies on ministry compiled by Cardinal Pellegrino, one of the world's renowned scholars on Saint Augustine. These homilies of Saint Augustine not only deal with an aspect of ministry which Augustine sought to bring to his day and age, but also reflect an ideal of ministry which has pervaded the Church for many centuries and has recently been reintroduced by the teachings of the Second Vatican Council in its conciliar decrees.

In this book, these sermons appear in English translation for the first time. The publication is so arranged that it is a meditation book rather than just a book for reading. It is especially important for all those connected with ministry — bishops, priests, deacons, and lay leaders — for the thought of Augustine will have a message for each of these as well as a general message for Christian living.

This book, published in the centenary year 1986/1987, which commemorates the 1600th anniversary of the Conversion of Saint Augustine, is a fitting tribute to a man like Augustine, who brought his conversion experience, his gift of grace, to the service of the people of his day through his ministry and his writings and who touches us today with his teachings and spiritual legacy.

I could not have produced this book in English without the help of Audrey Fellowes, the capable translator of these sermons. To her I am deeply indebted. I also wish to thank Mr. and Mrs. Paul Henkels for their financial support in this endeavor and for their constant interest in the writings of Augustine. May God bless all these people.

I ask that those who read this little book pray for the couple to whom it is dedicated, Howard and Jeanne Brass. May they rest in peace.

26 May 1986   John E. Rotelle, O.S.A.

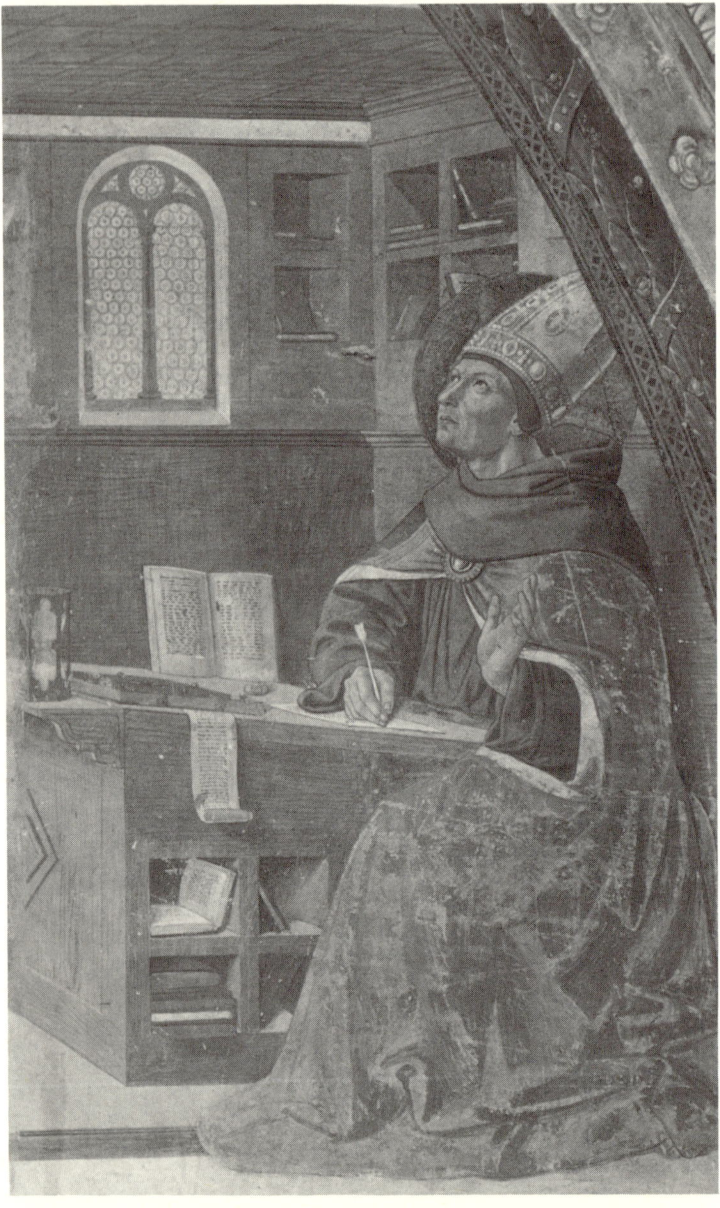

INTRODUCTION

The Priesthood As Service in Saint Augustine's Thought

For Saint Augustine the ministry of bishop is the source and center of every ecclesiastical ministry. If anyone would look through the numerous pages in which Saint Augustine explains the meaning of the ministry of bishop, and tried to find a guideline to explain and unify its manifold aspects and duties, it could easily be found in one of the concepts most familiar to the bishop of Hippo (and not only to him!): a bishop is the servant of God and of the Church.

Therefore, we think that a brief study of this motif may serve as a useful introduction to the reading of a selection of Augustinian texts which have as their common theme, intentionally or coincidentally, the person and mission of the shepherd of souls.

"I Am a Servant" (Servus sum)

Returning to one of the main concepts of several of the gospel parables, Saint Augustine speaks of the Church as a firm whose head *(paterfamilias)* is God, while the bishop plays the part of manager *(procurator)*, a "servant." In a sermon given toward the end of his life on the anniversary of his own consecration, to those complaining of the severity with which the bishop insists on the observance of the divine commandments, Augustine answers that as manager and servant it is not for him to be free with his promises, or to quieten consciences against the will of the one Lord (Sermon 339, 9).

The spiritual goods which the bishop distributes to the faithful are not his own but God's. He takes them from the divine "storeroom," since he is only God's servant, to share them with the faithful, his "fellow servants," who work in company with himself in their Lord's vineyard (Sermon 229E, 4).

Elsewhere he sees himself as the innkeeper to whom Christ, the Good Samaritan, entrusts the wounded man, giving him two silver coins and promising to refund him for anything he spends above that.

> All that we have to spend, my friends, is our Lord's money. We are your fellow servant; we live on the same food as we give to you. None must attribute to us the good they receive. We are bad servants if we give you nothing good, but if we give you good, it is not for us to make pretentious boasts, because we are not giving you anything of your own.

And he ends his sermon with a vigorous exhortation that they should love Christ and their neighbor: "We must all love him with our whole heart, and for him we must help each other. We all have one king; may we all reach the one kingdom!" (Sermon 179A, 8).

Servant, then, of God and Christ. Since Christ was willing to become the servant of humanity, the shepherd of souls can only serve him by putting himself at the service of the faithful: "You will serve Christ well if you serve those whom Christ has served." And a little further on he refers to the saying of Jesus: *Whichever of you wants to be the greatest must be the servant of the rest of you* (Matthew 26: 26). He tells his hearers, "He whose blood has made you free has made you my servant," and continues, "That is just what you ought to tell us, because it is true." Listen to him again: *We are your servants through Jesus* (2 Corinthians 4: 5), but in our Lord. May he grant us to serve you well. For whether we like it or not we are servants; but of course we want to be willing servants, loving rather than compulsory servants" (Commentary on Psalm, 103, sermon III, 9).

He later returns to this concept in a sermon given in Carthage at a bishop's ordination in 411 (Sermon 340A, 1-2).

It is to this principle that Augustine appeals in 412, to justify his intervention with the proconsul Apringius on behalf of the Circumcellions and the Donatist clergy guilty of serious offenses:

> I beg you not to consider me as inadvisedly meddling in your affairs. I am obliged to involve myself with every care on behalf of the Church entrusted to me. I am at its service and must see to its welfare, for I am not so interested in being at the head as in being useful — *non tam praeesse, quam prodesse* (Letter 134, 1).

Recommending manual labor to his monks, he regrets being unable to apply himself to this as he would like to, since he is prevented from doing so by ill health and by the custom of the Church, to whose service he is dedicated. And a little further on, he says "We are the servant of his Church, and especially of its weaker members... If you are brothers, if you are our own sons, if we are your fellow servant, or rather your servant in Christ, listen to our advice, keep our commands, and receive what we provide you with" (*The Work of Monks*, 37).

To forestall possible objections and the danger that the faithful might lose the respect due to a bishop if he were presented to them as their servant, Augustine, in the sermon at Carthage mentioned above, declares himself to be well aware of what is involved in such a task and such a responsibility.

Since it is of the utmost importance that bishop and faithful realize the relationship established between them by such a "service," Augustine, continuing to expound this theme, resolves the apparent paradox by showing that it is precisely in their duty to serve the Church that the reason for the preeminence conferred on bishops is to be found: *praesumus si prosumus*. In this brief play on words is contained one of the most essential chapters of pastoral theology, and it will rightly become the key concept in a tradition. We think of the Rule of Saint Benedict (64, 9) and above all that of

Saint Gregory the Great (I, 6).

Foundations

While Augustine delights in stating this concept by means of one of those innocuous stylistic devices so dear to classical rhetoric, he is well aware that he is expressing a truth founded on the word of God.

We have already cited some of the biblical texts to which he refers. But there is one Pauline passage relating directly to the office of bishop which Augustine expounds with particular care: *Whoever desires the office of bishop desires a noble task.* (1 Timothy 3: 1) "He wants to explain to us the exact nature of a bishop's office, which by its name indicates a task, not an honor... Therefore, while the love of truth seeks a holy quiet, the obligations of love take up the burden of a righteous employment" (*City of God,* 19, 19).

This is the sum of Paul's thought, as interpreted by one of the best of his modern exegetes. Since Christians were aspiring to various gifts of God, the Apostle advises them to desire rather the ungrateful task of governing the community. Here "task" *(ergon)* is a technical term which indicates "a task in God's service, for example, the 'building' of the Christian community, the sanctification of a soul, the fruit of apostleship." It is therefore a clear presentation of the priesthood as service of the Church: It is, as Father Spicq says, the "first appeal to vocations in the early Church."

Further on, the exegete just quoted develops the basic concept of the priesthood as service of God, which is apparent in general from the pastoral letters:

> Once committed, the priest is no longer free and can no longer dispose of himself; he has become the servant, the slave of God, bound to fulfill his master's orders, to carry out the task assigned to him; it is not only a question of the feeling of friendship for a beloved being, of keeping a promise and of self-respect, but also of strict obligation, of obedience without condition or reserve, of total dependence. The mentality of today, of souls even more devout but unconsciously influenced through and through by secular standards, finds it difficult to conceive this servile submission of humanity before its Creator. If God commands, no one can evade his orders. A priest, minister and slave of God, is particularly bound to obey his Lord's commandments; more than anyone else, he must have a sense of belonging to God. All the feelings of trust, love, and devotion which give him a new relationship with God are in a way secondary to the acceptance of this submission to a transcendent and omnipotent Master, who is entitled to demand everything of one he has created, without regard to the latter's preferences or personal desires.

For Augustine, the duty of serving the Church is only one aspect of the fundamental law of love, which must inspire the Christian's whole life.

To a bishop, Severus, who wrote to him with great admiration and said how much he would like to receive a long letter from him, he writes in answer: "It is precisely the duty of love to be useful to the brothers who are dear to us in Christ and, to the best of our ability, to help whoever turns to us for help." In this spirit he gives himself without sparing: "But I think that even you, my brother, know how many things I have on my hands. The various tasks connected with the service which I am bound to give *(nostrae servitutis necessitas)* leave me hardly a few moments free, and if I spend them on other things, it seems to me I am failing in my duty" (Letter 110, 5).

How To Serve

The basic conception of the priesthood as service is the source of a whole ascetic theology of the pastoral life, the characteristics of which Augustine outlines with a liveliness and realism which in his affirmations and exhortations reflect a daily experience lived and suffered.

Unselfishness is the disposition principally required of a shepherd of souls, who knows that he works not for himself but in the service of Christ and the Church. Such is the criterion by which Augustine resolves the problem resulting from the conversion of Donatist bishops and other clergy, who retained their rank when they were received into the Catholic Church: "They are received in the way that appears essential to the peace and benefit of the Church, for *we are not bishops for ourselves,* but for those to whom we administer the word and sacrament of the Lord." He then goes on to praise those bishops who, with a sense of holy humility, renounced of their own accord an office which they did not think they could fulfill in the requisite manner (Against Cresconius II, 11, 13).

Augustine is fond of contrasting the shepherd with the hireling using the criterion indicated by Saint Paul (Philippians 2: 21) to distinguish between them: the first thinks of the interests of Jesus Christ, the other of his own.

To the many texts quoted in these pages to explain this concept we may add a passage from a sermon on Psalm 103. The proper dispensers of truth and the sacraments of God are, like Peter and Paul, servants who

> do not look at what they give, because they are not selling the Gospel: they are giving it free, because they have received it free. They rejoice in your good works, because this is of use to you; they are not asking for your gifts, but are looking forward to the profit to yourselves (Commentary on Psalm 103, sermon III, 12).

The bishop's daily life conformed entirely to his teaching and, as his biographer Possidius has described it to us, was simple and frugal. Since he was wholly absorbed in the pursuit of spiritual matters, "it was quite an event if now and then he detached his thoughts from eternal matters to lower them to the level of earthly affairs" (Possidius, 24).

INTRODUCTION

It is becoming to a bishop, as the "servant of many," to possess the *humility* of a child. Christ recommended this virtue to the apostles who were eager for the first place. This concept is fully developed by Augustine in a sermon given at the ordination of a bishop, and in another sermon, written in the style of a commentary, on the allegory of the good shepherd. Both of the sermons are given in this collection.

Saint Augustine argues that according to the etymology of the Greek noun, a bishop *(episcopos)* is one who keeps watch from a height, like a watchman who guards the vineyard from an elevated position. "But the account we have to render from this raised place is in danger, unless we stand there so humble in heart as to be ourselves beneath your feet, and so humble as to pray for you, that he who knows your souls may keep watch over them" (Commentary on Psalm 126, 3).

Sincere humility will prompt the shepherd to have *respect* for souls. First of all, it is not a question of tactics, however intelligent, to make oneself agreeable to those one wants to gain for Christ, but rather a duty arising from the knowledge of one's vocation as a servant of Christ and the Church.

In the sermon just quoted, continuing his commentary on verse 1 of Psalm 126 — *Unless the Lord keeps watch over the city, those who guard it toil in vain* — Augustine remarks:

> We are your guardian because it is our duty to administer to your needs, but we ourselves want to be cared for in the same way as you. We are like a shepherd to you, but under that other Shepherd we are sheep like you. Because of our position, we are like a master to you, but under the one Master we are fellow pupils in this school of ours.

In the same way that slaves have to employ their time and labor doing their master's will and serving their master's interests, the shepherd must employ unlimited *devotion* in doing all he can for the souls to whose service he is assigned by the supreme Shepherd.

This is Augustine's policy: to serve the servants and children of God, those who are his own brothers and sisters and his own masters, with his heart and his spoken and written word (Confessions, 9, 37).

There was another bishop, a certain Audax, who, like the bishop Severus already mentioned, wanted a long letter from Augustine. The latter refused his request, alleging that the burden of work left him hardly a moment to reflect on the most important and urgent subjects which he must write about, and to restore the physical powers "necessary for the service which is incumbent on us" (Letter 261, 1).

One who was close to him admired the unceasing laboriousness with which he applied himself, day and night, in Hippo and beyond it. He tried to convince the Donatists (See Possidius, 9) by word of mouth and in writing. He listened patiently to the faithful who applied to his tribunal, "sometimes till the dinner hour, and sometimes going all day without food" (Possidius, 19). He worked by day and kept watch at night to meditate and to dictate his writings (Possidius, 24).

One cannot help but be moved by the conclusion of a sermon given on 18 December 425, when he was 71 years old. After lamenting the old age which he claims makes him wordy and dull, he declares that as long as God gives him the strength he will not abandon his people, and asks the faithful to pray for him, that up to the last he may be able to serve them by preaching God's word (Sermon 355, 7).

And so he did, according to the testimony of Possidius: "Up to his last illness he preached the word of God in church with assiduity, zeal, and vigorous intelligence" (Possidius, 31).

The service of Christ and of souls requires a devotion that remains steadfast even in the face of death. The long letter of 228 to Bishop Honoratus of Thiabe, who asked if the clergy ought to stay at their posts or flee when a district is invaded by the barbarians, is entirely founded on this principle: "Christ's servants, ministers of his word and sacrament, must act as he ordered or permitted." Anyone who is the target of a personal attack by persecutors is allowed to flee, "as long as the rest, who are not so directly attacked, do not abandon the Church, but administer nourishment to their fellow servants." Shortly after this he quotes the words of John (1 John 3: 16) somewhat freely: *As Christ gave his life for us, so we too must give our lives for our brothers and sisters.*

At the heart of this service, and the ultimate reason for performing a service which is given not in the spirit of a hireling but generously and willingly, is *love* — love for Christ, who entrusted his sheep (Sermon 147A, 1) to Peter only after hearing his thrice repeated assertion, *You know that I love you;* love for souls, members of Christ, redeemed by his blood" (Sermon 296, 33).

The idea of the "priesthood as service" is obviously not exclusively Saint Augustine's; he founds it on the word of God, to which he continually refers. If this view of the pastoral mission is one on which he lays particular stress, the history of the Church throughout the centuries is studded with the splendid figures of disciples who have devoted their entire lives to the generous service of Christ and their fellow Christians, from the pope, Saint Gregory the Great, *servus servorum Dei,* to Jean-Baptiste Vianney, the humble parish priest of Ars whose bishop, Monsignor De Langalerie, gave a funeral oration in his honor on 6 August 1859, with a commentary on the gospel text: *Euge, serve bone et fidelis* (Matthew 25: 23), applied in the liturgy to holy confessors and even popes:

> Jean-Baptiste Vianney, our holy parish priest of Ars, is a servant of God with seventy-four years

of good and faithful service to his credit, one who has devoted his entire life to the fulfillment of his sacred duties. As a boy, even when quite a child, he served God; as a student for the priesthood he served God; rejections failed to discourage him in his hopes of serving God more completely and usefully by entering the priesthood. Without doubt his only reason for wanting to be a priest was to serve God. He has well proved it: as priest, curate, and parish priest, he always served God.

As you know, this service ended by filling his life, to such an extent that the everyday actions which we perform and offer in indirect praise to God had almost disappeared from his life. He neither ate nor slept; this familiar saying had almost become true of him. Two or three ounces of food a day, and one or two hours of sleep were enough for him. And what did he do with the rest of his time? He was entirely at God's service, and the service of the souls entrusted to his care; fourteen, sixteen, eighteen hours a day spent hearing confessions; confession interrupted by catechism, which itself was such eloquent preaching that, even if one did not agree with it or could not understand it, his appearance in the pulpit, his appearance alone preached to one, moved and converted one. And how else did he spend his time? He stayed with his beloved parishioners, visited the sick, prayed long hours of prayer, read holy books: in a word, he spent the entire day in acts directly applied to the glory and service of God, and this day of absolute devotion to God began again and again without ceasing, Sundays and weekdays, day and night, without respite or holiday.

To cast a kind of luminous arc between the early centuries and our own times, let me end with the words of a shepherd of this century, Cardinal Giacomo Lercaro, the faithful echo of a tradition which is the glory of the Church in its constant teaching and above all in its example of generous devotion:

> It is for the salvation of your souls, you people of Bologna, that I have come to this city. My powers, my life, my time are for this. I have no wealth; I was born in poverty and have lived in poverty, and my intention, hope, and desire is to die in poverty. But what I have, what I suffer, what I am able to do is all for yourselves. I lay it at your feet and place it at the service of your souls. *I am your servant in Jesus Christ.*

Michele Pellegrino

CHAPTER 1

INTRODUCTION   While commenting on the gospel passage of the Good Shepherd, Augustine considers the meaning of various images which occur: shepherd, door, wolf, thief, etc. and dwells upon the figures of the shepherd and the hireling, instruments of one and the other which God uses so that his gospel of truth and salvation, either with good intentions or with secondary ones, may be preached.

Homilies on John's Gospel, 46

THE GOOD SHEPHERD

The Actors of the Parable

*W*hen our Lord Jesus spoke to his sheep, the present and the future who were both present at the time (for those who were to become his sheep were gathered together with those who were already his sheep), to his present and future sheep, then, to those and to ourselves, and to all who will become his sheep even after us, he revealed who it was who had been sent to them. And so all hear the voice of their shepherd, saying, *I am the good shepherd.* He would not have added the word *good* unless there were bad shepherds. And there are bad shepherds; they are thieves and robbers, or, as often happens, they are hirelings. We must examine all the characters our Lord has placed before us here, and distinguish between them and know who they are. For instance, he has now made two things clear to us which he had previously left obscure to a certain extent: we now know that he is the door, and we know that he is the shepherd. In yesterday's reading we were told who the thieves and robbers are, and the doorkeeper was mentioned as well; today we have heard about the hireling and the

THE GOOD SHEPHERD 17

wolf. Therefore, the door is among the good things, and so are the doorkeeper, the shepherd, and the sheep; among the bad are the thieves and robbers, the hirelings, and the wolf.

The Door and the Doorkeeper

We understand that our Lord Jesus Christ is the door and the shepherd, but who can we take to be the doorkeeper? He explained the first two to us himself, but left us to look for the meaning of the doorkeeper. And what does he say about the doorkeeper? *The doorkeeper lets him in.* Lets whom in? The shepherd. How does he let the shepherd in? By opening the door to him. And who is that door? The shepherd himself. If our Lord Jesus Christ had not explained, had not himself said, *I am the shepherd* and *I am the door* (John 10:3-9), would any of us dare say that Christ himself is both shepherd and door? If he had said, *I am the shepherd,* but not said, *I am the door,* we would have tried to discover who the door was, and perhaps have remained before the door, thinking it was something different. In his grace and mercy he explained that the shepherd was himself; he explained the door in the same way, but left us to look for the meaning of the doorkeeper. Who shall we say is the doorkeeper? Whomever we decide on, we must make sure that it is no one who might be thought greater than the door itself, just because the doorkeeper in the houses of this world are greater than the doors. In this world, the doorkeeper is ranked above the door, instead of the door above the doorkeeper, because it is the doorkeeper who guards the door, and not the other way around. However, I do not dare say that anyone is greater than the door, for I now know the meaning of the door. It is not kept secret from me; I am not abandoned to my own conjectures, nor am I allowed to think of it in human terms. God has spoken, truth has spoken, and what the unchangeable has said cannot be changed.

The Various Figures of Christ

I shall give you my own thoughts, then, on this profound subject; all may choose what seems best to them, yet their thoughts must be devout, as it is written, *Think of the Lord with righteousness and seek him with simplicity of heart* (Wisdom 1:1). Perhaps we ought to understand the doorkeeper as the Lord himself. For in our own world there is a much greater difference between a shepherd and a door than there is between a doorkeeper and a door; and yet our Lord called himself both the shepherd and the door. Why then should we not understand him as also the doorkeeper? Literally, our Lord is not a shepherd; nor is he a door, for no carpenter made him. If, however, by way of analogy he is both the door and the shepherd, then I venture to say he is also the sheep. A sheep, of course, is cared for by the shepherd, yet Jesus is both shepherd and sheep. Where is he found as the shepherd? Here, in

THE GOOD SHEPHERD

the words of the gospel — *I am the good shepherd* (John 10:11). Where is he the sheep? Ask the prophet — *He was led like a sheep to the sacrifice* (Isaiah 53:7). Ask the friend of the bridegroom — *Here is the Lamb of God, who takes away the sin of the world* (John 1:29).

There is something even stranger I must tell you concerning these analogies. The lamb, sheep, and shepherd are all friends, and shepherds are in the habit of guarding their sheep from the lion. Yet, though he is the sheep and the shepherd, we also read these words about Christ — *The Lion of the tribe of Judah has conquered* (Revelation 5:5). All these things, my friends, you must understand by way of analogy and not in a literal sense. We are used to seeing shepherds seated on a rock, watching from that position over the flocks committed to their care. The shepherd is superior to the rock on which he sits, yet Christ is both the shepherd and the rock (1 Corinthians 10:4).

All this is figurative. If you were to ask me for the literal truth about Christ, it is this: *In the beginning was the Word, and the Word was with God, and the Word was God* (John 1:1). If you were to ask me for the literal truth, it is this: He is the only Son, begotten of his Father from eternity to eternity, equal to his Father, and through him all things were made; he is unchangeable with his Father, unchanged even in assuming human form, man by incarnation, Son of man and Son of God. All this I have told you is not analogy but truth.

The Holy Spirit as the Doorkeeper

Let us be content, then, my friends, to understand by way of certain analogies that he is the door and the doorkeeper. For what is the door? Our means of entry. Who is the doorkeeper? The one who opens the door for us. Who, then, opens himself, if not he who tells us who he is?

Our Lord had told us he was the door, but we had not understood. While we were uncomprehending, he remained closed to us, and the one who opened the way to our understanding is the doorkeeper. Therefore, there is no need to look for anything else — no need, but perhaps there is the desire. If so, you must stay on the right road and remain with the Trinity. If you look for someone else as the doorkeeper, you ought to think of the Holy Spirit, for the Holy Spirit will not disdain to be the doorkeeper when the Son has seen fit to be the door itself. You may perhaps see the Holy Spirit as the doorkeeper; in speaking of the Holy Spirit, our Lord himself told his disciples, *He will teach you all the truth* (John 16:13). What is the door? Christ. Who is Christ? Truth. Who opens the door, if not he who teaches all truth?

Who Are the Hirelings?

But what can we say of the hireling? He is not mentioned among the good.

THE GOOD SHEPHERD

The good shepherd, our Lord says, *gives his life for the sheep. But the hireling, because he is not the shepherd and the sheep are not his own, abandons the sheep and flees when he sees the wolf coming, and so the wolf plunders and scatters the sheep* (John 10:12). The hireling plays a bad part here and yet he is not entirely useless; he would not be called a hireling unless someone employed him and paid for his services. Who, then, is this hireling, who deserves reproach but is also indispensable? Here indeed, my friends, our Lord himself must enlighten us, so that we may understand the hireling and avoid being one ourselves. Who, then, is the hireling? In the Church there are certain people in positions of authority of whom the apostle Paul says, *They seek their own ends, not those of Jesus Christ* (Philippians 2:19-21). What does it mean, *they seek their own ends*? It means that they do not love Christ for nothing, they do not seek God for the sake of God; they pursue worldly rewards, their eyes are fixed on gain, and they long to be honored by their fellow creatures. One in authority who loves such things and serves God for the sake of them is a hireling and not to be reckoned among the children of God. Our Lord says of such people, *I tell you truly, they have received their reward* (Matthew 6:5).

Listen to what the apostle Paul says of the faithful Timothy:

> I hope, in the Lord Jesus, to send Timothy to you very soon, that I may derive courage from

learning how things go with you. I have no one quite like him for genuine interest in whatever concerns you (Philippians, 2:19-21).

The shepherd lamented in the midst of hirelings; he looked for someone who would sincerely love Christ's flock, and found none of the same mind as himself among those who were with him at the time. The meaning is not that in the Church of Christ's time there was no one except the apostle Paul and Timothy who really cared about the flock; it just so happened that when he sent Timothy, he had none of the children of God who shared his outlook and was stranded in the midst of hirelings *seeking their own ends, not those of Jesus Christ.* And yet in his genuine care for the flock, he preferred to send one of God's children and to remain himself among the hirelings.

We meet with hirelings, too, but only our Lord can distinguish them; he who looks into our hearts is the one to distinguish them. Yet we can sometimes become aware of them, for it is not without reason that our Lord himself said about wolves, *You will know them by their fruits* (Matthew 7:16). Trials put many to the test, and at such times their thoughts are revealed, but many remain unknown.

Our Lord's sheepfold must have its overseers, both children of God and hirelings. But the overseers who are children of God are the shepherds. If they are shepherds, how can there be one shepherd unless they are all members of the one shepherd, whose own sheep they are? They are also members

THE GOOD SHEPHERD

of the one sheep, because *he was led like a sheep to the sacrifice.*

Grape Among the Thorns

But you must learn that hirelings, too, are essential. There are indeed many in the Church who pursue earthly advantages and yet preach Christ, and Christ's voice is heard through them. The sheep follow not the hireling but the voice of the shepherd speaking through the hireling. Listen to our Lord's own description of the hirelings: *Scribes and Pharisees occupy the chair of Moses; you must obey their instructions, but not follow their example* (Matthew 23:1). What did he mean, if not: Listen to the voice of the shepherd through the hirelings? Seated in the chair of Moses, they teach God's law; therefore, God teaches through them. But if they should prefer to teach their own ideas, you must shut your ears to them and do nothing they tell you to do, for such people certainly seek their own ends, not those of Jesus Christ. Yet no hireling has dared to tell Christ's people, seek your own ends, not those of Jesus Christ, for they do not preach from Christ's chair the evil they do. The harm they inflict comes from their bad actions, not from their good instructions. Beware of the thorn when you pluck the grape.

I am glad you have understood, but for the sake of the less quick-witted, I shall be plainer on the subject.

How could I say, beware of the thorn when you pluck the grape, when our Lord asks, *Are grapes gathered from thorns, or figs from thistles?* (Matthew 7:16) It is entirely true that they are not, yet what I said, beware of the thorn when you pluck the grape, is also true, for sometimes the grape springing from the root of the vine hangs over a hedge, and as the vine shoot grows, it becomes entangled among thorns, and so the thornbush bears fruit which is not its own.

It is not the vine that has produced the thornbush, but the vine shoot that has become embedded among thorns. Look only for the roots. Look for the root of the thornbush, and you will find it outside the vine; look for the origin of the grape, and you will see that it springs from the root of the vine.

Therefore, the chair of Moses was the vine; the customs of the Pharisees were the thorns. True instruction given by bad people is the vine shoot in the hedge, the grape among thorns. Pick carefully to avoid scratching your hand while you are looking for fruit and to avoid copying the bad ways of those whose good instructions you listen to. *You must obey their instructions,* pick the grapes; *but not follow their example,* beware of the thorns. Listen to the shepherd's voice even through hirelings, but avoid being hirelings yourselves, since you are members of the shepherd. Listen to the holy apostle Paul, who said, *I have no one who really cares about you; for all seek their own ends, not those of Jesus*

Christ (Philippians 2:20). When elsewhere he distinguished between hirelings and children of God, observe what he said: *Some preach Christ through envy and strife; but others also through good will; some from love, knowing that I am ready to defend the gospel; but others also proclaim Christ through obstinacy, with no pure motive, thinking to stir up trouble for me in my imprisonment* (Philippians 1:17).

These were hirelings, and they envied the apostle Paul. For what reason did they envy him, if not because their aims were worldly? But pay attention to what he adds: *What does it matter, as long as Christ is proclaimed in every way, in pretense or truth; and I not only rejoice at this, but shall continue to rejoice* (Philippians 1:18).

Christ is truth; let truth be proclaimed in pretense by hirelings and in truth by the children of God. The children patiently wait for their Father's eternal inheritance; the hirelings are in a hurry to get their worldly reward from their employer. As for my own human glory, which I see the hirelings envy, may it decrease, and yet may the divine glory of Christ be proclaimed far and wide by the tongues of both hirelings and children of God, since *Christ is proclaimed both in pretense and in truth.*

One Shepherd and Many Shepherds

We have seen who is the hireling. Who is the wolf, if not the devil? And what is said of the hireling? *When he sees the wolf coming, he takes flight because the sheep are not his own, and he does not care about the sheep* (John 10:11).

Was the apostle Paul like this? Certainly not. Was Peter? No. Were the rest of the apostles, except Judas, the son of perdition? No. They were shepherds then? To be sure, they were shepherds. And how is there one shepherd? I have already told you — because the shepherds were members of one shepherd. They rejoiced in the head, were united under that head, and lived with one spirit in the unity of one body; in that way, they all belonged to one shepherd. If, then, they were shepherds and not hirelings, why did they take to flight when they suffered persecution? Explain this to us, Lord. I have read in Paul's letter that he fled — he was lowered down the wall in a basket to escape from his pursuers (2 Corinthians 11:33). Did he care nothing for his sheep, whom he abandoned at the wolf's approach? To be sure, he cared for them, but entrusting them in prayer to the shepherd seated in heaven, he saved himself by flight in their own interests, as he says elsewhere, *For your sake I must remain on earth* (Philippians 1:24). All know that the shepherd himself said, *If they persecute you in one town, flee to another* (Matthew 10:25). May our Lord see fit to explain this subject to us. Lord, you told those whom you certainly wished to be faithful shepherds and whom you formed to be your members, *If they persecute you, flee*. Therefore, you wrong the hirelings when you blame them for

THE GOOD SHEPHERD 27

taking flight when they see the wolf coming. We entreat you to answer this profound question for us. Let us knock; the doorkeeper will be there to open himself, because he is himself the door.

The Flight of the Hireling

Who is the hireling who sees the wolf coming and takes flight? The one who seeks his own ends, not those of Jesus Christ, and who does not dare accuse the sinner openly (1 Timothy 5:20). Here are some who have sinned, and sinned gravely; they ought to be rebuked, they ought to be excommunicated, but excommunication will turn them into enemies who lie in wait and do harm whenever they can. The one who seeks his own ends, not those of Jesus Christ, is already silent and refrains from reproach for fear of losing what he pursues — human friendship — and of incurring the vexation of human enmity. Here was the wolf seizing the sheep by the throat, the devil persuading the faithful to adultery, and you keep silent instead of reproaching; you hireling, you saw the wolf coming and fled. He answers indignantly: Look, I am here, I have not fled. You fled because you were silent; you kept silent because you were afraid. Fear is mental flight. You stood in body but fled in spirit, which was not the action of the one who said, *Though absent in body, I am with you in spirit* (Colossians 2:5). For in what way did he flee in spirit who, even when absent in body, reproached by letter those guilty of fornication? Our emotions are the movements of our minds. Joy is an expansion of the mind; sadness, a contraction; desire, an advance; and fear, mental flight. When you are pleased, your mind expands; when you are worried, it contracts; when you long for something, it advances; and when you are afraid, it takes flight.

There is a reason given for the flight of the hireling when he sees the wolf. What is that reason? Because he does not care about the sheep. And why is that? Because he is a hireling. What do you mean, *he is a hireling*? He seeks a worldly reward, and so he will never inhabit an eternal home.

There are still points here to be examined and discussed with you, but I have no wish to overburden you. We provide our fellow servants with the Lord's food; we feed the sheep in our Lord's pastures and are fed together with them. As we must provide what is necessary, so we must not burden the less intelligent with too much food for their minds. Therefore, I would ask you not to take offense if I refrain from discussing today all the points which I believe remain to be discussed here; the same reading will be read to us again, in the name of the Lord, on a day when a sermon is to be given, and will, with his help, be more carefully explained.

CHAPTER 2

INTRODUCTION   This sermon, given in Carthage around 411 on the occasion of the ordination of a new bishop, is considered one of the best on this theme: The mission of the bishop is a service to God and neighbor in the spirit of love and humility. Praesumus, sed si prosumus *(a difficult phrase to translate into the vernacular): We will be good leaders of the flock if we know how to be useful to the flock. The bishop puts his life at the disposal of souls to the point of sacrificing his life for them as Jesus and Peter did.*

Sermon 340A (Guelferbytanus 32)

THE BISHOP'S MISSION

Bishop, Servant of Many

This is the third sermon we have given you since God thought fit to lead me to you, but in the past two days you have heard what should most concern you. Today, by the grace and mercy of God, your bishop is ordained, and therefore we must say something to exhort ourselves, to instruct him, and to teach you. What must first be understood by one who is set over the people is that he is the servant of many. He must not disdain this; he must not, I say, disdain to be the servant of many, for the Lord of lords did not disdain to serve us. Once, indeed, from the dregs of worldliness, a desire for supremacy had stolen upon the disciples of our Lord Jesus Christ, our apostles, and their sight was clouded by a vision of exaltation. As we read in the gospel: *A dispute arose among them as to which of them was the greatest* (Luke 20:24). But our Lord was present and, like a physician, checked their swelling. And when he saw the vice that had given rise to their quarrel, he stood a child before him and said to his disciples, *Only one who has become like this child will enter the kingdom of heaven* (Matthew 18:3). He praised

THE BISHOP'S MISSION 31

humility in a child. He did not intend for his followers to have the minds of children; as the Apostle says elsewhere, *Do not be childish in your outlook. Be like children as far as evil is concerned, but in mind be mature* (1 Corinthians 14:20).

Pride is a great evil; it is even the foremost evil, the beginning, root and cause of all sin. It was pride that overthrew the angel and made the devil. And even when overthrown, he passed on the cup of pride to upright humanity. He aroused pride in the human being who had been created in the image of God, and that pride made humanity shameful. The devil envied humanity and persuaded Eve to defy God's law and use her own power.

And how did he persuade her? *If you eat,* he said, *you will be like gods* (Genesis 3:5). Consider, then, whether it was not pride that persuaded her. The two who had been created human wanted to be gods. They assumed what they were not and lost what they were; they did not lose their human nature, but they lost blessedness, both present and future. They lost the place to which they were to be raised, deceived by one who had been thrown down from there.

CHAPTER 2

Invitation to Humility

Therefore, in the reading we have just listened to, when the apostle Paul mentioned among other things the virtues of a bishop, he added, *He should not be a new convert,* new, as it were, to the faith, *lest he become conceited and thus incur the punishment once meted out to the devil* (1 Timothy 3:6). What does it mean, incur the devil's condemnation? Not to be judged by the devil, but condemned with the devil, for the devil will not be our judge. Because he erred through pride and pride made him wicked, he will be condemned to eternal fire. Anyone, he says, who is given a high place in the Church must be careful not to become exalted with pride and thus incur the same condemnation as the devil. Therefore, when our Lord spoke to the apostles to confirm them in holy humility, after he had shown them a child as an example, he said to them, *Whoever wants to be greatest among you must be your servant* (Matthew 20:27).

There you see that I have not wronged my brother, your future bishop, in wishing and urging him to be your servant. If I wronged him, I wronged myself first, for in speaking about a bishop I speak not just as anyone but as a bishop. What I urge him to do, I myself fear, remembering the words of the holy Apostle, *I do not run as if in uncertainty: I do not fight as if beating the air; but I punish my body and keep it in subjection, for fear that I who preach to others may be found unfit to do so* (1 Corinthians 9:26-27).

Servants Like Jesus

Therefore, to put it briefly, we are your servants — your servants, but also your fellow servants. We are your servants, but all of us have one Lord. We are your servants, but for Jesus' sake, as the Apostle says, *We are your servants for Jesus' sake* (2 Corinthians 4:5). Through him we are servants, and through him we are also free; it is he who tells those who believe in him, *If the Son sets you free, you will be truly free* (John 8:36). Shall I hesitate, then, to be a servant through him, since unless I become free through him I should remain lost in slavery? We have been placed at the head and we are servants. We are in command, but only if we are useful.

In what way, then, is the bishop who is put in command a servant? In the same way as our Lord himself. When he said to his apostles, *Whoever wants to be greatest among you must be servant to the rest* (Matthew 20:26-27), he quickly consoled them, for fear that human pride might take offense at the word servant, and by giving himself as an example encouraged them to do what he had commanded. *Whoever wants to be greatest among you must be servant to the rest* (Ibid.). But observe how he did this: *As the Son of man came not to be served but to serve* (Matthew 20:28). Let us see what his service meant. If we look at material service, we see that his disciples served him, but it was he who sent them to buy food and prepare rooms for them to eat in. Similarly, it is written in the gospel that when the day of his passion drew near, his disciples asked him, *Lord, where do you wish us to prepare for you to eat the passover?* (Matthew 26:17) And so he tells them where it is to be prepared, and they go and prepare and are his servants. What does he mean, then, when he says, *The Son of man came not to be served but to serve?* Listen to what follows: *He came not to be served but to serve, and to give his life as a ransom for many* (Matthew 20:28).

This is the meaning of our Lord's service. That is the kind of servant he commanded us to be. He gave his life as a ransom for many; he redeemed us. Which of us is fit to redeem anyone? It is his blood, his death that has redeemed us from death, his humility that has raised us from the ground, but we too have to make our own small contribution to his members, because we have been made his members. He is the head and we are the body.

The apostle John also urges us in his letter (1 John 3:16) to follow the example of our Lord, who had said, *Whoever wants to be greatest among you must be your servant, in the same way that the Son of man came not to be served but to serve, and to give his life as a ransom for many* (Matthew 18:27-28). John urges us to do the same, saying, *Christ laid down his life for us: so we also ought to lay down our lives for each other.*

Our Lord himself, after his resurrection, asked Peter, *Peter, do you love me?* Peter answered, Yes. Three times the same question was asked, and the same answer was given each time; all three times our Lord added, *Feed my sheep* (John 21:15). How do you show me that you love me, if not by feeding my sheep? What will you give me by loving me, since you hope for everything from me? Here is something, then, for you to do in your love for me: *Feed my sheep.* This is repeated three times. *Do you love me? Yes.* Then *feed my sheep.* Peter had denied the Lord three times in fear, so three times he acknowledged him in love. Next, when our Lord had entrusted his sheep to him for the third time, he told Peter, who in answering and acknowledging his love had condemned and destroyed his fear, *When you were young, you girded yourself and went where you liked; but when you are old, another will gird you and take you where you do not wish to go. He said this to indicate by what kind of death he would glorify God* (John 21:18). He foretold that his own cross and passion would also be Peter's. Go that way, the Lord says, and *Feed my sheep,* that is, suffer for my sheep.

Bishop in Name and Deed

That is the sort of person a good bishop ought to be; otherwise, he is no bishop. What use is it to an unfortunate man to have the name Lucky? If you saw a miserable beggar whose name was Lucky and addressed him by his name, saying, Come here, Lucky; go there, Lucky; get up, Lucky; sit down, Lucky — then, despite his name, he would continue to be unfortunate. Something similar happens when you address a man as bishop who is not a bishop at heart. What does the honor of the name bring him, except a heap of reproach?

But who is the bishop who is called a bishop and is not one? He who rejoices in that honor rather than the salvation of God's flock, who in that high office seeks his own ends, not those of Jesus Christ. He is called a bishop but is not a bishop; the name is of no use to him, but no one calls him anything else. Have you seen the bishop? Have you greeted the bishop? they ask. Where have you come from? The bishop. Where are you going? To the bishop.

Therefore, to be worthy of his name, let him listen not to me but with me — let us listen together, and as fellow pupils in one school let us learn together from the one master, Christ, whose chair is in heaven, because it was first the cross on earth. He has taught us the way of humility, descending to ascend, visiting those who lie in the lowest depths, and raising those who wanted to be united to him.

Jesus, Teacher and Example of Humility

Listen now very carefully. Two of our Lord's disciples, the brothers John and James, the sons of Zebedee, longed more than the rest to share his sublime position, and because they were ashamed to tell him themselves, they sent their mother to speak for them. *Lord,* she said, *in your kingdom, let one of my sons sit at your right hand and the other at your left* (Matthew 20:21).

THE BISHOP'S MISSION

But our Lord answered, speaking to them and not to their mother, *You do not know what you are asking.* And he added, *Can you drink the cup that I must drink?* (Matthew 20:22) What cup does he mean, if not the one of which he speaks at the approach of his passion: *Father, if possible, let this cup pass from me* (Matthew 26:39)? Can you, he asked, drink the cup which I am going to drink? And immediately, in their eagerness for his sublimity and forgetfulness of their own infirmity, they answered, *Yes.* Then he said to them, *You will indeed drink my cup, but to sit at my right or left is not mine to give you; it has been prepared for others by my Father* (Matthew 20:23). For whom has it been prepared, if not for his disciples? Who will sit there, if not his apostles? It has been prepared for others, not for you; for others, not for the proud. He gave them a good example of humility himself, in saying, *It has been prepared for others by my Father,* since he certainly prepared himself what he said was prepared by his Father, so that even here he might not appear arrogant and fail to encourage them toward humility, which was his concern in all he said here. For the Father prepares nothing which the Son does not prepare, nor does the Son prepare what the Father does not; our Lord himself says, *I and my Father are one* (John 10:30), and, *Whatever the Father does, the Son does likewise* (John 5:19). He is our teacher of humility by word and act; for by word, through the mouths of angels and prophets, from the beginning of creation he has never failed to teach us humility. He has also thought fit to teach us by his own example.

Our Creator came humbly among us, as one created, he who created us and was himself created for us, God before all time, man in time, to set us free from time. He came as the great physician to heal our pride. From east to west the human race lay sick like a great patient in need of a great physician. At first, the physician sent his assistants, but afterward he came himself, when some were in despair of him. Our own physicians send their assistants to treat what appears to be a simple case, but they go themselves when the patient is in great danger. The human race, overwhelmed by every vice, was in great danger, flowing especially from the fountain of pride; therefore, our Lord came himself to cure that pride by his own example.

Humankind, for whom God humbled himself, you should be ashamed to go on being proud. It would already have been great humility for God to be born for you, but he even thought it fit to die for you. So he hung on the cross in his human nature as his persecutors, the Jews, shook their heads before the cross and said, *If he is the Son of God, let him come down from the cross, and we shall believe him* (Matthew 27:40-42). But he preserved humility, and therefore did not come down. He had not lost the power, but he wanted to show endurance; just think of his very power and might and you can imagine how easily he who could rise again from the grave could have come down from the cross. But if humility and

THE BISHOP'S MISSION

endurance were not shown to you, they could not be commanded from you. And if they were to be commanded by word, they had to be shown and commanded by example. Therefore, let us pay attention to this in the Lord. Let us observe his humility, drink the cup of his humility, keep to that cup, and reflect on it. It is easy to think of sublime matters, easy to delight in honors, easy to give ear to toadies and flatterers. But to endure abuse, listen patiently to reproach, pray for those who insult us — this is our Lord's cup, this is our Lord's feast. *Are you invited by one greater than you? Remember, you must prepare the same* (Proverbs 23:1).

The Office of Bishop Is a Noble Task

In his description of a bishop, the Apostle says this first: *Whoever longs for the office of bishop desires a noble task* (1 Timothy 3:1). What does this mean? Does it look as if he has stirred up all to desire the office of bishop, who will do better to be ambitious rather than modest, and do better to get by arrogance something which is not even their due than avoid in fear something which is certainly due to them?

No, it means nothing like this. He is not teaching us to canvass for the office of bishop. But you must try to understand what he said, if I can explain my own thoughts on the subject. The Apostle's meaning is clear to the intelligent but as dark as night to the proud and ambitious. Well, then, what the Apostle says is, *Whoever longs for the office of bishop desires a noble task.* To long for the office of bishop is not to long for the office of bishop; it is to desire a noble task.

But what about the man who does not want to perform a noble task but works for himself — does he want to be a bishop? No, he does not long for the office of bishop. As I said earlier, what he seeks is the name, not the reality. I want to be a bishop — if only I were a bishop! If only you were! Are you in search of the name or the reality? If you want the reality, you desire a noble task. If you want the name, you can have it even if you perform your task badly, but with the consequence of a worse punishment. What shall we say then? Are there bad bishops? No, there are not. I venture to say with absolute certainty, there are no bad bishops, because if they are bad, they are not bishops. Again you remind me of the name, and say to me, he must be a bishop, for he sits in the bishop's chair. Even the watchman in the vineyard can be made of straw.

Bishop as a Father

He said, among other things, that the bishop should be *married only once* (1 Timothy 3:2), but how much better would it be for him to never marry? You are forbidden, he said, to have more than one; but how much better if not even one. *Having obedient children* (1 Timothy 3:4) means that if he has any children, he should make them obedient, not that he should try to have children if he has none. He approved of discipline for children, so as to keep order in the home — *For if a man does not know how to manage his own home, how will he care for God's Church?* (1 Timothy 3:5) Those are the Apostle's own words. And how will the bishop be childless if he is a good bishop? So your own bishop in Christ's name, helped by the grace of Christ, has chosen not to have earthly children, in order to have spiritual children. It is for you to submit to him and obey him in a fitting manner, and serve him faithfully; he will then have obedient children, a great many instead of a few, heavenly instead of earthly, co-heirs instead of heirs.

Praise, the Number One Danger

We have talked about good bishops and bad bishops. We have told you what bishops ought to be, and what they ought to avoid being. But what does this mean to you, God's people? It means something to you, too, for we want you to be built on rock, to rise as a temple for God, to become fit to receive God, not to waver in uncertainty but to place your hope in unshakable truth.

Whatever we are like, you must be safe. It is indeed a good thing that we who are placed at your head are obliged to be good bishops, and not only bishops in name. This is good for us, for a great reward is promised to such bishops. But if we were not like that, but bad, which God forbid, and sought honors for ourselves, neglected God's commands, and thought nothing of your salvation, punishments greater than the promised rewards would await us. Let this never happen to us, and you must pray for us. The higher our position, the greater is our danger. For we think of the account we must give of the obedience of the people and of their insults. Many obey us; many slander and speak evil of us. We are put in greater danger by those who obey than by those who insult us, for the obedience of those beneath us rouses our pride, while their insults exercise our patience. In the one case I fear a fall, in the other I strengthen my defenses. One of God's servants tells me, *Do not be afraid when people reproach you* (Isaiah 51:7). Our Lord Jesus Christ also says, *You will be blessed when people revile you and say all kinds of evil things falsely against you because of me* (Matthew 5:11). If in reviling you they tell the truth, they do not speak ill because they tell the truth; it is those who tell lies who speak ill. But what is it our Lord has promised us? *Rejoice and exult, for you have an abundant reward in heaven* (Matthew 5:12). Whoever slanders me increases my reward, but those who flatter me wish to diminish it. But what shall I say, my friends? Must we desire you to be abusive, to make our reward greater? No, we do not wish our own reward to be increased by your evil. Be blessed and obey; let us be in danger rather than you be diminished. What, then, if the people should meet with a bad bishop?

Our Lord, the bishop of bishops, has made sure that your hope should not depend on any human

THE BISHOP'S MISSION

being. Here I speak to you as a bishop in our Lord's name. What sort of person I am, I do not know; how much less do you? I can understand in some way what up to now I have been, but as to what I shall be at some later date, is there any way I can know that? As Peter presumed to, and his real self was revealed to him, he did not know he was sick, but his sickness was not hidden from the physician. In his presumption Peter dared promise, *I am ready to go with you to death. I shall lay down my life for you* (John 13:37). And the physician looked deep into Peter's heart and answered, *Will you lay down your life for me? I tell you truly, before the cock crows you will deny me three times* (John 13:38).

Hope in God, Not in Humanity

With your prayers to help us, may the Lord grant us to be, and continue to be to the end, what all of you who wish us well want us to be, and what he who has called and appointed us wants us to be. May he help us fulfill his commands.

Whatever we are like, your hope must not be in us. As a bishop, I say this to my own disparagement, but I want to rejoice on your account, not to be made proud. If I find people placing their hope in me, I cannot congratulate them at all. They must be corrected, not confirmed; changed, not supported. If I cannot warn them, it saddens me; if I can warn them, I am no longer sad. Just as now I speak to God's people in Christ's name, I speak in God's

Church, I speak as God's servant, whatever kind of person I am. Your hope must not be in us; your hope must not be in humanity. Whether good or bad, we are ministers. If we are good, we are faithful ministers and truly servants. Pay attention to what we administer. If you are hungry and do not wish to be ungrateful, notice from whose store it is that you are provided with food. As to the kind of dish in which the food you are eager to eat is offered to you, this should not concern you. *In the great house, which belongs to the head of the family, there are not only gold and silver dishes, but also earthenware* (2 Timothy 2:20). So the dish may be silver, gold, or earthenware, but what you must be concerned with is whether it contains the bread, and whose bread it is which is distributed to you by his own gift. Notice who it is I am speaking about, by whose own gift this bread is distributed to you.

Christ is the bread — *I am the living bread who came down from heaven* (John 6:51). Therefore, we distribute Christ to you on behalf of Christ; we distribute Christ as Christ's servant, that he may come to you. He must himself be the judge of our ministry. If the bishop is a thief, from this chair he must never tell you to commit theft; he must only tell you not to steal, for this is what he receives from the Lord's store. If he chooses to tell you something different, you must reject it and tell him, This does not come from the Lord's store; you are speaking to me in your own name. *When he tells lies, he speaks with his own voice* (John 8:44). Therefore, let him

THE BISHOP'S MISSION

tell you what God commands — You must not steal, commit adultery, or murder; let him tell you that God commands you to be fearful instead of proud, to turn away from the love of the world, and to place your hope in the Lord. Let him teach you these commands of God. If he himself fails to comply with them, what is that to you? The Lord your God is Christ, and he has made you safe. *The Scribes and Pharisees,* he says, naming them as symbols of authority, *have succeeded to the chair of Moses; you must do what they tell you to do but not what they do, for they teach one thing but do another* (Matthew 23:3).

What are you going to say to this? What excuse are you going to find for yourself at your judgment before Christ? You will say, I did wrong because I saw that my bishop was not living a good life. Christ will answer you, You chose a companion to lead you to condemnation, instead of one to lead you to freedom. You copied the bad life of your bishop. Why did you copy him, rather than listen to me through him? Did I not tell you in my gospel that when you see that your superiors are bad, you should do what they tell you to do but not what they do? You should have listened to me through them, and you would not have been lost through them.

Do What They Say, Not What They Do

If, then, even the words of the bad can be good, we must now answer Christ and say to him, not with contempt or reproach but because we are in search of the truth: Lord, if the words of the bad can be good — for which reason you warned and commanded us to do what they say but not what they do — if, then, the words of the bad can be good, why do you say elsewhere, *Hypocrites, your words cannot be good, since you yourselves are bad* (Matthew 12:34)? You must look at the problem carefully, until with his help you find its solution.

I state it again: Christ says, Do what they say but not what they do, for they say one thing but do another. What does this mean, then, if not that their words are good but their actions bad? And therefore we must do what they say, not what they do. Elsewhere he says, *Are grapes gathered from thornbushes, or figs from thistles?* (Matthew 7:16)

Every tree is known by its fruit (Luke 6:44). How shall we obey? How shall we understand? Here are brambles and thorns. And you are told to act. Lord, you command me to gather grapes from thorns. In one place you command me, in another you forbid me. How shall I obey you? Listen, try to understand. When I tell you to do what they say but not what they do, pay attention to what I said before that: They have succeeded to the chair of Moses. When their words are good, it is because they are spoken not by themselves but by the chair of Moses. He

THE BISHOP'S MISSION

meant the chair to stand for teaching; it is not that the chair speaks, but the teaching of Moses. It is contained in their memories but has no place in their actions. But when they themselves say anything, when they themselves speak, or rather, when they speak in their own voices, what do they hear said to them? *How can your words be good, since you yourselves are bad?* There is another analogy to which you must pay attention: Do not gather grapes from thornbushes, for thornbushes can never produce grapes.

But have you not noticed a vine shoot growing in a hedge, becoming covered with thorns, coming into bud among thorns, and producing grapes? You are hungry, and you pass by and see grapes hanging among the thorns. You do nothing; you leave them alone. Or, you are hungry and decide to pick them. Pick them, but put out your hand carefully and warily; pick the fruit, but beware of the thorns. So, too, when someone who is very bad preaches Christ's teaching to you, listen to it, take it in, and do not despise it. If the preacher is a bad person, the thorns are his own; if his words are good, they are the grapes hanging among thorns, not the fruit of thorns. Therefore, if you are hungry, pick the grapes, but look out for the thorns, for if you copy what he does while willingly listening to his words, you have put out your hand incautiously. You have run into the thorns before reaching the fruit; you leave, scratched and torn. The fruit produced by the vine is then no longer of any use to you; the thorns produced by their own root stand in your way. To avoid being cheated, you must pay attention to where you have picked the fruit from. There is a vine shoot there. Look at the vine shoot and see how it belongs to the vine, how it springs and grows from it, but runs into thorns. Should the vine, then, restrain the vine shoots? So, too, has Christ's teaching, as it has grown and advanced, intermingled with good trees and bad thornbushes; it is preached by both the good and the bad. You must see where the fruit comes from; trace it back to its proper source to determine what feeds you and what pricks you. Outwardly they are mixed together, but their roots are different.

CHAPTER 3

INTRODUCTION The anniversary of Augustine's ordination as a bishop causes him to reflect, with renewed fervor of good intentions, on the meaning of the mission which has been entrusted to him. The office of bishop is certainly difficult, but the grace of God and the prayers of the faithful accompany him.

Sermon 340

ORDINATION ANNIVERSARY

Pray for Me

The cares of my office have been a cause of anxiety to me since the day on which that burden was placed on my shoulders, of which I have to give a rigorous account. But I am much more deeply moved by thoughts of this kind when the anniversary of that day revives the memory of the original occasion and reminds me that I should hold the office I received then as if I came to receive it today. But what is to be dreaded in this office, if not the fear that we should delight more in the dangers of our high position than in what is useful to your salvation?

You must come to my help, then, with your prayers, that our Lord may think fit to bear his burden with me. When you pray, you pray for yourselves, too, for this burden of mine, of which I am speaking, what else is it but you? Pray rightly, as I pray, that you may not be a heavy burden to me. For our Lord Jesus would not have called his burden light, unless he helped us carry it. But you yourselves must support me, so that, as the Apostle commands, we may bear each other's burdens and thus fulfill the law of Christ (Galatians 6:2).

Servant and Fellow-Servant

Unless the Lord helps us carry our burdens, we shall sink beneath them, and unless he carries us, we shall fall to our death. My position at your head frightens me, but the condition I share with you consoles me. I am a bishop set over you, but a Christian in company with you. The first is the name of the office I have undertaken, the second of grace; the first of danger, the second of salvation. So it is as if we are tossed about by a storm in the raging sea of that office, but as we remember who has redeemed us by his blood, it is as if we enter the safety of a harbor in the stillness of that thought. Though this office is hard work for us personally, the common benefit provides us with rest.

So if the fact that I have been redeemed with you delights me more than the fact that I have been set over you, then, as our Lord commands, I shall be more tirelessly your servant, for fear of being ungrateful for the redemption which made me worthy to be your fellow-servant.

Pastoral Ministry Is an Act of Love

Indeed I ought to love my Redeemer, and I remember what he said to Peter: *Peter, Peter, do you love me? Then feed my sheep.* Three times he asked the same question and gave the same command. His love was examined, a task imposed on him — for the greater the love, the lighter the task. *What shall I give the Lord in return for all he has given me?* Even if I say I repay him by feeding his sheep, it is the grace of God with me, not I myself, which does this. Therefore, where shall I be found returning a benefit, since I am forestalled everywhere? And yet, because we love him for nothing, because we feed his sheep, we expect a reward. How will this happen? How is it consistent to say, I love him for nothing so that I may feed his sheep, and I demand a reward for feeding them?

This could never happen; we would never seek a reward from him whom we love for nothing, unless he whom we love was himself the reward. If we try to repay him for our redemption by feeding his sheep, how shall we repay him for having made us shepherds? For it is our own badness that makes us bad shepherds, and may we never be that, but it is only by his grace that we can be good shepherds, and may he grant that we always be that. Therefore, my friends, *we warn and entreat you not to receive God's grace in vain.*

You must make our office fruitful. You are the field that God cultivates. Outwardly you receive the one who plants and waters, but inwardly you receive the one who makes it grow. We must reproach the restless, encourage the timid, support the weak, confute our opponents, beware of the treacherous, teach the ignorant, rouse the lazy, restrain the contentious, check the proud, make peace among the quarrelsome, help the needy, free the oppressed, approve the good, tolerate the bad, and love all. In this great, many-sided, and varying office with its different concerns, you must help us with your prayers and your obedience, so that we may delight not so much in being set over you as in being useful to you.

Let Us Pray Together

Just as it is to your advantage that we should pray devoutly for God to be merciful to you for your salvation, so you too ought to pray to the Lord for us. Let us not think unsuitable what we know the Apostle has done. He so longed to be commended to God in prayer that he begged all the people: *pray for us also* (Colossians 4:3). And, therefore, all that we say must serve to encourage ourselves as well as to teach you. Just as we must reflect with great fear and anxiety on how we may fulfill the office of bishop without blame, so must your own care be to strive to be humbly obedient to all the commands given to you.

Therefore, my very dear friends, let us pray together that my office of bishop may be useful to both myself and you. It will be useful to me if I tell you what you ought to do, and to you, if you do what I tell you. If we continually pray for you, and you for us, with perfect Christian love, then with our Lord's help we shall happily come to eternal blessedness.

CHAPTER 4

INTRODUCTION   *The following discourse was given by Augustine on one of his anniversaries of ordination as a bishop. It is almost an examination of conscience which he makes aloud and openly and by which he reminds himself of his duties and responsibilities.*

The responsibility of office weighs on Augustine and suggests to him warnings and exhortations, addressed especially to the lost sheep of his flock. One notes in the words of the preacher a popular and pastoral tone especially in the fact that the simple things of daily life bring with them profound spiritual meaning.

Sermon 339

THE SHEPHERD'S CROSS

Rendering an Account

This day, my friends, reminds me to consider the burden of my office more attentively, and although I think of it each day and night, somehow this anniversary brings it so forcibly to my mind that I cannot at all avoid thinking about it. As the years go on, or rather, as they recede, and bring us nearer to the last day, which is bound to come at some time, the more the thought distresses and torments me as to what kind of account I can give about you to our Lord God. There is a difference between each one of you and ourselves, in that you will have to give an account precisely of yourselves alone, but we must account for ourselves and for all of you as well. Therefore, although our burden is greater, if we carry it well it brings greater glory, but carried unfaithfully it throws us headlong into the most frightful punishment.

What then must I do, today most of all, if not tell you of my danger, so that you may become my joy? But it would be dangerous for me to pay attention to the way you praise me and shut my eyes to the way you live. But he, in whose sight I speak, or rather in whose sight I think, knows that I am not so delighted by popular praise as troubled and grieved by the lives of those who praise me. Moreover, I do not wish to be praised by those who live badly. I abhor and detest it; it is pain, not pleasure, to me. On the other hand, if I said I do not wish to be praised by those who live well, it would be a lie, but if I said I wish to be praised, I am afraid of being more eager for the shadow than for the substance.

So what am I to say? I am neither entirely willing nor entirely unwilling. I am not entirely willing, for fear of the danger in human praise; I am not entirely unwilling, for fear of ingratitude in those to whom I preach.

I Have Appointed You Watchman

It is my burden you heard described to you just now, when the prophet Ezekiel (Ezekiel 33:2-11) was read to you. It is not enough that the day itself reminds us to consider the same burden; we also have a scriptural passage read to us, of a kind to strike great fear into our heart, so that we may think about the burden we carry. Unless he who imposed it helps us carry it, we sink beneath it.

This is the passage you heard: *If I bring the sword to a land, and the people appoint a watchman for themselves to look out for the sword's coming and announce it, and the watchman is silent when the sword comes, so that the sword falls on sinners and kills them, those sinners will indeed die for their own wickedness, but the watchman will answer for their death. But if he sees the sword coming, and the trumpet sounds, and he announces it, and the people to whom he announces it ignore it, they will indeed die in their wickedness, but the watchman will have saved his own life. And so you, son of man, I have appointed you watchman for the children of Israel* (Ezekiel 33:2-7). He has explained the sword, the watchman, and the death he meant; he has not allowed us to make the obscurity of the reading an excuse for our carelessness.

Therefore, he says, *I have appointed you watchman. If I tell sinners they will certainly die, and you keep silent and they die in their sin, then they will indeed die in their sin* as they rightly deserve, *but you will answer for their deaths. But if you tell sinners they will certainly die, and they take no notice, they will die in their wickedness, but you will have saved your own life* (Ezekiel 33:7-9).

God Wishes the Conversion of the Sinner

He adds a message which he wanted the people of Israel to hear. *Therefore, you must tell the children of Israel: What is it you say among yourselves: Our wickedness weighs on us, we are wasting away in our sins, how can we live? The Lord says this: I do not wish the death of the wicked as much as that the wicked should return from their perverse ways and live* (Ezekiel 33:10-11).

He wanted us to pass this message on to you. If we fail to do so, we are going to give a bad account of our position as watchman. But if we give you the message, we shall have done what concerns us. In your eyes we are already safe. But in what way are we safe, if you are in mortal danger? We do not wish our own glory to be won at the price of your punishment. Safety has indeed been given to us, but love makes us anxious. And so we tell you, and you know that I have always told you, you know that I have never kept it from you. *As I live, says the Lord God, I swear I take no pleasure in the death of the wicked, but rather in the wicked person's conversion, that he may live* (Ezekiel 33:11). What were the wicked saying? We are told the words of the impious and evil: Our crimes and our sins weigh us down, we are rotting away because of them. How can we survive? (Ezekiel 33:10) The sick are desperate, but the physician promises hope. People ask themselves, How can we survive? God answers, You can survive. If all are liars (Psalm 115:1), God alone is truthful; then let everyone blot out his own words, and write down God's. You must not despair; you can survive, not by your past badness but by your future goodness. You will blot out your evil actions if you abandon evil. Everything good or bad is blotted out by change. If you have turned from a good life to a bad one, you have blotted out the good. Consider what you care about, and what you obtain: two stores are prepared for you. You will find what you have put there. God is a faithful guardian; he will give you back what you have done.

Despair and Presumption

There are others who are not lost in despair; they do not say to themselves, *Our crimes and our sins weigh us down, we are rotting away because of them, how can we survive?* They deceive themselves in a different way: they flatter themselves that, thanks to God's great mercy, they need never fear correction. They say, Although we do wrong, even if we commit sin, even if we live dissolute and criminal lives, even if we despise the poor and needy, even if we are swollen with pride, even if we feel no regret for our evil deeds, is God going to destroy such a multitude to save a few? So there are two dangers: one which we have just heard described in the reading from the prophet Ezekiel, and the other of which the Apostle has not failed to warn us.

As regards those who are dying in despair, as if doomed to fall by the sword like gladiators, whose worthless lives are full of a greed for pleasure, and who despise their own lives as almost condemned already, the prophet tells us what they say to themselves: Our crimes and our sins weigh us down, we are rotting away because of them; how can we survive? But it is with the other danger in mind that the Apostle says, *Do you despise his wealth of goodness, mercy, and patience?* (Romans 2:4) Then

THE SHEPHERD'S CROSS

there are those who say, God is good, God is merciful; he will not destroy such a multitude of sinners to save a few, for certainly they would not be alive if he did not wish them to be, since though they do so much evil they go on living; certainly if God were displeased with them, he would immediately remove them from the earth. As regards such people the Apostle says, *Do you not know that God's kindness is an invitation to you to repent? In spite of this, your hard and impenitent heart is storing up retribution for that day of wrath when the judgment of God will be revealed, when he will repay us the reward our actions deserve* (Romans 2:4-6).

The Treasure of Good Works

To whom does he say this? To those who say, God is good, he will not take vengeance. He will give each of us precisely what our actions deserve. And you, what do you do? You store up. What do you store up? Wrath. Heap wrath upon wrath, and build up your store. What you store up will be returned to you; he to whom you entrust it will not defraud you. But if you put good actions into the other store, the fruits of righteousness, self-restraint, virginity, or conjugal chastity; avoiding deceit, homicide, and crime; remembering the needy because you too are in need; and remembering the poor because you are poor yourself; however rich you are, you are clothed in the rags of a human body. If thinking and acting thus, you put something good into the store for the day of judgment, then he who defrauds no one and who will give each of us the reward our actions deserve will say to you: Take what you put there, for there is plenty; when you put it there it was lost to your sight, but I kept it as I would give it back to you. Truly, my friends, when we put something in store we know that we put it there, but once placed there it is hidden from our eyes. Dig yourself a storeroom in the ground, with a narrow opening through which you can put things into the storeroom. You put in what you gradually acquire, and it remains there, out of sight. If the earth keeps your hidden possession safe for you, will he not do the same who made heaven as well as earth?

The Gospel Frightens Me

Therefore, my friends, you must lighten my burden and help me carry it — you must live good lives. Today we have our fellow-paupers to feed, and we must share our provisions with them, but as for you, these words of mine are your food. I have not enough to feed all with the bread which can be handled and seen. I feed you with what I feed on myself; I am a servant, not the head of the family. What I set before you comes from the same source that I live on myself, from our Lord's storeroom, from the feasts given by that head of the family who *for us became poor, though he was rich, that we ourselves might become rich by his poverty* (2 Corinthians 8:9).

THE SHEPHERD'S CROSS

If I set bread before you, after the bread was broken you would each take away a tiny piece of it. Even if I put out a great quantity, each of you would get very little. But as for what I say now, all of you possess the whole of it, and each of you possesses the whole of it. Have you divided my words into syllables to be distributed among you? Have you taken away a few words each from a long sermon? Each of you has heard the whole. But you must be careful of how you have listened to it, for I am a distributor, not a collector. If I failed to pay out money, but kept it to myself instead, the gospel would frighten me. I could say, Why should I be a nuisance to people, saying to the wicked, Stop your wicked behavior, you must live thus, act thus, and give up acting thus? Why should I be a burden to people? I have accepted the way I myself must live. I shall live as I am ordered to, as I am commanded to. Let me affirm what I have accepted. Why should I give an account of others? The gospel frightens me.

No one could love more than myself a more secure and tranquil life — nothing is better, nothing more pleasant than to explore the divine treasure in quiet surroundings. It is pleasant and good. Instead, preaching, reproving, correcting, teaching, and doing one's best for everyone is a heavy burden and a laborious task. Who would not shun such a task? But the gospel frightens me.

A servant came and said to his master, *I knew you were a troublesome man, reaping where you have not sown* (Luke 19:21). I have kept your money; I did not want to spend it. Take what is yours. If there is anything missing, punish me; if it is all there, leave me alone. But he answered, *You good-for-nothing servant, your own words condemn you* (Luke 19:22). Why is this so? You said I was greedy, so why have you not tried to make a profit for me? But I was afraid to use the money, in case I lost it. Is this what you say? People often complain, Why blame me? and your words are wasted on them; they refuse to listen to you. I, too, he said, did not want to use your money, for fear of losing it. But he was told, *You should at least have put my money on deposit, so that when I returned I could have claimed it with interest* (Luke 19:23). I appointed you to be a distributor, he was told, not a collector; you should have busied yourself with distribution and left the collecting to me.

The Foolishness of the Obstinate Sin

In this fear, then, let everyone consider how to receive. If I distribute in fear, should those who receive feel safe? May those who were bad yesterday be good today. That is my distribution, that those who were bad yesterday may be good today. They were bad yesterday, but did not die; if they had died in their sins, they would have gone to a destination from which they would never have returned. Yesterday they were bad, today they live; may life be of use to them; may they not live badly.

Why do they want to add today's evil to yesterday's? You want to have a long life, but not a good one? Who would put up with anything long and bad, even a dinner? Are you so hardened in mental blindness, is your own heart so deaf, that you want everything you possess to be good except yourself? Is it a country house you want? I refuse to believe you want a bad one. You are only content with a good wife and a good house. Need I run through everything one by one? You do not want a bad pair of shoes, but you want a bad life? As if bad shoes hurt you more than a bad life! When a bad, tight pair of shoes hurts you, you sit down, take them off, and either throw them away, correct them, or change them, to make sure your toes feel comfortable, so that you can wear your shoes. You care nothing about correcting a bad life, by which you lose your soul. But I see clearly where the origin of your mistake lies: an ill-fitting shoe gives you pain, a badly lived life gives you pleasure. One hurts, the other pleases. But what pleases for a time is more painful later. On the other hand, what is a temporary, salutary pain gladdens you later with boundless pleasure and overflowing joy.

The Rich Man and Lazarus

Consider the joyful man and the man in pain — one rich and the other poor; the rich man feasting, the poor man tormented; the rich man in an honored position and attended by slaves, the poor man licked by dogs; the one refreshed with feasts, the other unable even to satisfy his hunger with crumbs. Pleasure and poverty passed; the rich man's happiness and the poor man's misery vanished. Unhappiness followed for the rich man and happiness for the poor man. What was past was beyond recall; what followed was to last for eternity. The rich man burned in hell, the poor man rejoiced in Abraham's bosom (Luke 16:19-31). Earlier, the poor man had longed for a crumb from the rich man's table; later, the rich man longed for a drop of cold water from the tip of the poor man's finger. The poverty of one ended in the fullest abundance; the pleasure of the other turned into endless pain.

Thirst has followed after feasts, pain after pleasure, fire after the purple robe. This is the feast that Lazarus was seen to enjoy in Abraham's bosom. It is what we wish you all to enjoy and to enjoy with you ourselves. For what feast would it be that we gave you, if we invited you all, and the church was full of tables at which everyone was eating and drinking? These are the pleasures of the moment. Think over what I am telling you, so that you may come to those feasts which you are to enjoy forever.

No one disturbs these feasts, nor are the feasts themselves such that they feed us with their own destruction and refresh us to their own loss. They will be unimpaired, even while they refresh us. If our eyes feed on light without loss to light, what kind of feasts will those be, spent in the contemplation of truth, in the sight of eternity and the praise of God, with our happiness secure, with steadfast mind and immortal body, with no old age to destroy our bodies or hunger to weary our souls? There no one grows greater or less; there no one is born because no one dies. There you are not urged to undertake any of the tasks which we exhort you to do now.

The Eternal Banquet

You have just heard our Lord's words, which he addressed to all of us: *When you give a banquet, you must not ask your friends to it* (Luke 14:12). He indicates to you the people to whom you ought to be generous. *You must not ask your relations, who are able to repay you; rather, you must invite the poor, the weak, the blind, the crippled, and the needy* (Luke 14:13), none of whom can repay you. And will you lose by it? *It will be returned to you at the retribution of the righteous* (Luke 14:14). You must pay out, he says; it is I who receive, note down, and return. God has told us this and exhorted us to do this, and promises to repay us.

Since he repays us, who will rob us? *If God is for us, who is against us?* (Romans 8:31) When we were sinners he gave us Christ's death; will he deceive us if we live righteously? Christ did not die for the righteous, but for the wicked. If God has given his Son's death to the wicked, what has he in store for the righteous? What is he keeping for them? He can keep nothing better for them than what he gave for them. What did he give for them? *He did not spare his own Son* (Romans 5:6). What is he keeping for them? His very Son, but as God who is to be enjoyed, not as a man who is to die. That is what God invites you to enjoy.

How do you hear him call you? Where, by what way, and how are you thought worthy to hear him? When you come, will you clearly be told, *You must share your bread with the hungry; you must clothe those you see destitute* (Isaiah 58:7)? Is this passage read to you: *When you give a banquet you must invite the crippled, the blind, those in need and the helpless* (Luke 14:12)? There will be no one helpless there, no one crippled, no one blind, no one weak, no stranger, and no one destitute; all will be sound in body, all vigorous, all living in abundance, and all clothed in eternal light. What stranger do you see there? It is our native land. We are strangers here on earth; let us long for that land of ours. Let us obey the commands, so as to demand the promises. Or — I have not put it well, I correct what I said — rather than to demand the promises, we shall receive what is spontaneously given to us. For if we demand, it looks as if God is unwilling to give. He will certainly give and will deceive no one.

Divine Generosity

Consider this, my friends. Look at the many blessings our Lord God gives to the bad — light, life, health, springs, fruit, children, and often honors

THE SHEPHERD'S CROSS

and the heights of power. All these blessings he gives to both good and bad. Can we think he keeps nothing for the good, when he gives such great blessings even to the bad? Let no one be persuaded to think so.

My friends, God keeps great blessings for the good, but they are *what no eye has seen, nor ear heard, nor human mind has thought of* (1 Corinthians 2:9). You cannot conceive of them before you receive them; you can only see them when you receive them. To think of them before you receive them is impossible. What is it you wish to see? It is neither a lyre nor a flute; it is not a sound that gives you pleasure to listen to. What do you wish to think of? It is nothing the human mind has thought of.

And so what do I do? I do not see, hear, or think. What do I do? You must believe; faith is a great means, a great receptacle in which you may receive a great gift. You must prepare yourself a receptacle because you will be going to a mighty fountain; so prepare yourself a receptacle. How do you prepare? Let your faith grow, let it become greater and stronger; it must be neither uncertain nor worthless, nor must it be broken but rather forged by the troubles of this world. But when you have acted and acquired faith, like a receptacle which is useful, capacious, and strong, God will fill it.

Indeed, he will not speak to you as people speak to one who implores them, Give me some wine, I beg you. They would answer, Yes, come, and I shall give you some. And so the other brings his jug and says, I have come as you told me to; and they exclaim, I thought you would bring a cup; why have you brought that jug, what have you come to do? I cannot afford to give you so much. Take away that jug you have brought, which is too big, and bring something small. Bring me something suitable to my limited means.

God does not speak like this. He is full and you will be full, and when he has filled you, his own fullness will still be intact. God's gifts are plentiful; there is nothing like them to be found on earth. Believe, and you will prove it true, but not now. When, you ask? *Wait for the Lord, be firm, and let your heart take courage,* so that when you have received his gifts you may say, *You have filled my heart with joy* (Psalm 26:14).

Do Not Despair or Presume

Wait for the Lord, be firm, and let your heart take courage, and so wait for the Lord. What does it mean, Wait for the Lord? It means that you may receive his gifts when he gives them, instead of demanding them when you want them. The time for giving has not yet come; he has waited for you, and so you must wait for him.

What do I mean by, He has waited for you, and so you must wait for him? If you already live righteously, if you have already turned to him, if you

THE SHEPHERD'S CROSS

dislike your past and are already pleased to have chosen a good new life, you should not hurry to God with your demands. He has waited for you to change your bad life; you must wait for him to crown your good life. If he had not waited for you, there would have been no one to give anything to. You must wait for him, then, because he has waited for you.

But you who do not wish to be corrected; whoever there is here who does not wish to be corrected yet — as if there was only one of you! I ought rather to have said, Whoever there is here, if there is anyone here, who has decided to be corrected; yet let me speak as if to one — Whoever does not wish to be corrected, what do you promise yourself? Are you perishing in despair or in hope? If you are perishing in despair, you say this to yourself: My crimes and sins weigh me down, I am rotting away because of them, how can I survive? Listen to the prophet's words: *I take no pleasure in the death of the wicked, but rather in the wicked person's conversion, that he may live* (Ezekiel 33:11). Or are you perishing in hope? What does it mean, perishing in hope? You say this to yourself: God is good, God is merciful, he forgives all our sins, he will not return evil for evil. Listen to the Apostle's words: *Do you not know that God's kindness is an invitation to you to repent?* (Romans 2:4) What remains, then? You have at least done something, if my words have found their way to your heart. I see what your answers are: The truth is, my despair is not such as to lead me to perish by it, and my hope is not so wrong as to lead me to perish by it. I do not say to myself, My crimes and sins weigh me down, I no longer have any hope; nor do I say to myself, God is good, he will repay no one with evil. I say neither one nor the other. I am impressed by the prophet, impressed by the Apostle. And so what do you say? Let me live the way I want to for a little longer. Those are the people who weary us. There are very many of them; they are a great trouble to us. Let me live the way I want to for a little longer; afterward, when I have reformed myself — the prophet's words are certainly true, *I take no pleasure in the death of the wicked, but rather in the wicked person's conversion, that he may live* (Ezekiel 33:11) — when I am converted, he will blot out all my sins. So why not add something to my pleasures, living as much as I want to, in the way I want to, and afterward returning to God?

Do Not Put Off Conversion

Why do you say this, my friend, why? Because God has promised to forgive me if I change myself. I see, I know, he has promised forgiveness; he promises it through his holy prophet and through me, the least of his servants. His promise is true — he has promised it through his only Son. But why do you want to add evil days to evil days? Let the evil of one day be enough for it (Matthew 6:34).

THE SHEPHERD'S CROSS

There is yesterday's evil, there is today's evil, and again there is tomorrow's.

Do you think your days are good when you satisfy your desires, when you nourish your heart through riotous living, when you set traps for another's chastity, when you defraud and distress your neighbor, when you deny that anything has been entrusted to you, when you are bribed into giving false witness, when you treat yourself to a good dinner? Therefore, you think your days are well spent? How can the day of a bad person be well spent? Do you want to add evil days to evil days?

I ask to be allowed time, you say. Why? Because God has promised me forgiveness. But no one has promised you life tomorrow. Or read to me — as you read the prophet, the gospel, and the Apostle to me, where they say that when you are converted God blots out all your sins — so read to me where you are promised a tomorrow, and then go and live badly tomorrow.

Yet, my friend, I ought not to have said this to you. You may have a long life; if so, may it be good. Why do you want to have a long and evil life? Either you will not have a long life, and that long life which has no end is bound to delight you. Or you will live long, and what evil will it be that you have lived a good life for a long time? You wish to live a long life that is bad instead of good, yet no one has promised you a tomorrow. You must reform. Listen to what

Scripture tells you. To prevent your despising me as just a man who is celebrating his anniversary, I quote to you from Scripture: *Delay not your conversion to the Lord* (Sirach 5:8). Those words are not my own, and yet they are mine; they are mine if I love the Lord. You must love the Lord yourselves, and they will be yours too. What I am saying now is Holy Scripture. If you despise it, it is your enemy. But listen to our Lord's words: *Make friends with your enemy quickly* (Matthew 5:25).

What does that formidable saying mean? You have come here to rejoice; today is called your bishop's birthday. Should I say anything to make you sad? On the contrary, I say it so that one who loves the Lord may rejoice, and that one who despises him may be angry. It is better for me to make the despiser angry than to deceive the faithful.

Dangerous Lethargy

All must listen while I read you the words of Scripture. You with your wicked delaying and your wicked grasping at tomorrow, listen to our Lord's words, listen to the preaching of holy Scripture. From my position above you I am the watchman. *Delay not your conversion to God, put it not off from day to day* (Sirach 5:8). Consider if he has not seen, and seen deep, into the hearts of those who say, I intend to start a new life tomorrow, but today I shall live badly. And when tomorrow comes, you will say the same again. *Delay not your conversion to the Lord, put it not off from day to day, for suddenly his wrath flames forth; at the time of vengeance, you will be destroyed* (Sirach 5:8-9). What have I done? Can I blot that out? I am afraid of being blotted out myself. Can I keep silent about it? I am afraid of being silenced myself. I am compelled to preach; in my own terror I am to frighten others. You must share my fear with me, so as to share my joy with me.

Delay not your conversion to God. Lord, observe that I am preaching your words. Lord, you know that you frightened me when your prophet was read; Lord, you know the fear I felt, seated in that chair, when your prophet was read. This is what I tell you — *Delay not your conversion to God, put it not off from day to day, for his anger will come suddenly, and in the time of punishment he will utterly destroy you.*

I do not want him to destroy you; I do not want you to say to me, I want to perish. I do not want you to perish — my "I do not want" is better than your "I want." Let us say you were a young man attending your old father who was sick, and he lay sick and lethargic in your arms, and the physician said to you, Your father is in danger; that sleepy state of his could be fatal. You must watch him carefully and keep him from sleeping. If you see him falling asleep, shout at him. If shouting is not enough, try shaking him. If even that is not enough, you must use painful means to prevent your father from dying.

You would attend him, but as a young man burdensome to an old one. He would start sinking into a pleasant sickness, closing his eyes beneath the weight of lethargy, and you would begin to shout at him not to sleep. He would say, I want to sleep, and you would answer, But the physician has said, If he wants to sleep, he must not be allowed to. And he would repeat, I beg you, let me alone, I want to die. But I do not want you to die, you say, the son to the father, even though he certainly desires to die. And yet you want to postpone your father's death, to live as much longer as you can with your old and dying father. Our Lord cries aloud to you, Do not sleep, for you may sleep forever; wake up, so that you may live with me, and have a father whom you will never have to carry to the grave. But you are deaf to him.

Vigilance and Prayer

What, then, have I done as a watchman? I am free; I do not oppress you. I know there are some who will ask, what did he want to tell us? He has frightened, oppressed, and blamed us. On the contrary, I have wanted to free you from blame. It is horrible and disgraceful; I do not want to tell you that your lives are evil, dangerous, and destructive, but it is disgraceful that I should deceive you, since God does not deceive me.

Our Lord threatens the wicked with death — the utterly worthless, the deceivers, the vicious, the adulterers, the pleasure-seekers, those who despise him, those who complain of the times and refuse to change their ways. Our Lord threatens such people with death, hell, and eternal destruction. Why do they wish me to promise what he does not? Supposing the agent offers you security? What use is that to you if the head of the house forbids it?

I am an agent, a servant. Do you want me to tell you, Live as you like, for our Lord will not destroy you? The agent has offered you security, but the agent's security is worth nothing. If only our Lord would offer it to you, and I could make you anxious to obtain it! Our Lord's security is valid even if I disown it, but mine is worthless if our Lord disowns it. But what is security, my friends, either mine or yours, if not listening to our Lord's commands with careful attention and faithfully waiting for what he has promised us?

In these actions in which we weary ourselves because we are human, let us implore his help and lament to him. We must not pray for the things of this world that pass quickly and vanish like smoke. We must pray for righteousness itself to be fulfilled and for sanctification in God's name. We must pray not for victory over our neighbor but for victory over our own desires, not for the satisfaction but the subduing of our avarice. Let our prayers be for this — to help us in our spiritual struggle and to obtain the crown of victory for us.

CHAPTER 5

INTRODUCTION   This sermon, given at Carthage, seems to have been delivered in the first years of Augustine's episcopate. Augustine treats of the themes of harvest of which Jesus speaks and of the precepts that Jesus gave to the sowers of his word.

Even with some forced exegetical passages we find concepts with a singular profundity and concreteness. Augustine is solicitous about his mission, realizing how sublime and difficult it is. He gives his all — mind and heart — to this mission.

The bishop has to sow, plant, cultivate, and prepare the earth, all in a spirit of love and fidelity to his mission. The Lord keeps watch over his work and blesses the labor of pastor and faithful.

Sermon 101

THE HARVEST

The Word of God

In the gospel passage which has just been read to us we heard of a harvest, and we feel obliged to ask what harvest our Lord means when he tells us, *The harvest is great, but the laborers few. Ask the Lord of the harvest to send laborers to gather his crops* (Luke 10:12). It was at that time that he added to his twelve disciples, whom he also called apostles, a further seventy-two and sent them all, as is clear from his words, to gather the harvest which was ready to be gathered.

What, then, was that harvest? It was not among the Gentiles, where no seed had been sown. So we are left to understand that the harvest was among the Jews. That was the harvest which the Lord of the harvest came to gather and to which he sent his reapers, while he sent not reapers but sowers to the Gentiles. Therefore, we must understand that the harvest was ready for gathering among the Jews, but was being sown among the Gentiles. It was out of that first harvest that the apostles were chosen, where (since it had to be gathered) the crop was already ripe; it was already ripe because the prophets

THE HARVEST

had sown the seed there first. It delights us to observe the cultivation of God's field and to rejoice at his gifts and at the laborers in his field. It was one who worked in the cultivation of this field who said, *I have worked harder than all of them* (1 Corinthians 15:10). But he was given the strength for the work by the Lord of the harvest, and so he added, *It is not I, but the grace of God with me* (1 Corinthians 15:10). He showed well enough that he was engaged in the cultivation of God's field when he said, *I planted, and Apollos watered* (1 Corinthians 3:6).

This is the Apostle who changed from Saul to Paul — that is, from the highest to the least, for he is named Saul after Saul the king, but "paulus" means small in Latin. Therefore, he was, in a way, interpreting his own name when he said, *I am the least of the apostles* (1 Corinthians 15:9). So Paul — that is, the smallest and the least — was sent to the Gentiles. He tells us that he was sent specially to the Gentiles. He writes this and we read, believe, and preach it. So he himself tells us, in his letter to the Galatians (Galatians 2:1-2, 9), that after he had been called by the Lord Jesus, he came to Jerusalem and discussed the Gospel with the apostles, and that they shook hands with him as a sign that both sides were in complete agreement. Then he says they decided among themselves that he would go to the Gentiles and they to the circumcised — he as the sower and they as reapers. Even the Athenians, without knowing it, called him by his right name, for when they heard him preaching, they asked, *Who is this sower of words?* (Acts 17:18)

Two Harvests

Pay attention, then, and share my delight in observing the cultivation of God's field and its two harvests, the one ready to be gathered and the other still to come, the one ready to be gathered among the Jews and the other ready to come among the Gentiles. Where can we find proof of this, if not in the Scripture of God, the Lord of the harvest? We have it here in the present passage, where we are told, *The harvest is great, but the laborers few. Ask the Lord of the harvest to send laborers to gather his crops* (Luke 10:2). But because in that harvest there were likely to be Jews who were opponents and persecutors, he said, *I am sending you, like lambs into the midst of wolves* (Luke 10:3). Let us show you something clearer on the subject of this harvest, which appears in the gospel according to John.

At the well where our Lord sat down to rest, great mysteries took place, but the time is too short for us to deal with all of them. But you must listen to what pertains to our present inquiry. We have undertaken to show you the harvest among the people to whom the prophets preached. The prophets were the sowers so that the apostles could be the reapers. The Samaritan woman was speaking with our Lord Jesus, and when, among other things, our Lord told her how God ought to be worshiped, she said, *We know that the Messiah will come, he who is called Christ, and that he will teach us everything.* And our Lord answered her, *I am he, I who am speaking with you.* Believe what you hear. Why ask about what you see? *I am he, I who am speaking with you.* But what she had said was, *We know that the Messiah will come,* whom Moses and the prophets announced, *he who is called Christ* (John 4:25-27).

Already there was an ear of corn ripening for the harvest. The harvest which was to be produced had received the prophets as sowers, and now the ripe corn was waiting for the apostles as reapers. As soon as she heard his answer she believed it; she left her water jar and quickly ran to announce the Lord.

The disciples had gone to buy bread at that time, and on their return they were amazed to find the Lord speaking with the woman. Yet they dared not say to him, What or why are you speaking to her? They kept their amazement to themselves and hid their daring in their hearts. So the name of Christ was not new to this Samaritan woman — she was already waiting for him to come, and she already believed he would come. Where had she gotten this belief from, unless Moses had sown it? Listen to these more precise words. Our Lord then said to his disciples, *You say that summer is still a long way off, but lift up your eyes, and see the fields shining for harvest* (John 4:35). Abraham, Isaac, Jacob, Moses, and the prophets have labored; they labored to sow the seed. The Lord, at his coming, has found the harvest ripe. The reapers, sent armed with the scythe of the gospel, have carried the sheaves to the Lord's threshing-floor, where Stephen was to be threshed.

Paul Sows the Word

Here Paul arrives and is sent to the Gentiles. And he is not silent in commending the grace which he received as a special and personal gift. He tells us in his writings that he was sent to preach the gospel where Christ's name was unknown. But now, because that first harvest has been gathered and all who were left were Jews, let us give our attention to our own harvest, for we have been sown by the apostles and the prophets. Our Lord himself has sown us, because he too was a reaper, for he was among the apostles. They were nothing without him, but he is complete without them. He himself told them, *For without me you can do nothing* (John 15:5). So when Christ was already sowing the seed among the Gentiles, what did he say? *A sower went out to sow* (Matthew 13:3). On the former occasion it was reapers who were sent out to reap, but here a diligent sower went out to sow. Why should it frighten him that some of the seed fell on the path, some on stony places, and some among thorns? If he had feared these difficult lands, he would not have reached the good land.

What is it to us, what use is it now for us to argue about the Jews or discuss the chaff? The only thing that matters to us is not to be the path, the stone, or the thorns, but to be the good land — *Our hearts are ready, Lord* (Psalm 57:8) — to yield thirtyfold, sixtyfold, and a hundredfold (Matthew 13:23). One is less and another is more, but it is all wheat. And so our hearts must not be the path, where the seed is trodden underfoot by passersby, where the enemy can snatch it away like a bird. They must not be a stone, where the seed will sprint up quickly in the sparse covering of earth, but is soon withered by the sun. They must not be thorns, which means full of worldly desires and the cares of a vicious life, for what is worse than the care of a life which does not allow us to reach life? What is more wretched than to lose life in our care for life? What is more unhappy than to fall a victim to death in our fear of death? We must root out the thorns and prepare the field, receive the seed and arrive at the harvest, and long for the barn rather than fear the fire.

The Bishop — Sower and Steward

Therefore, it is our concern, whoever we are whom our Lord has appointed laborers in his field, to say these things to you, to sow, plant, water, dig around any trees, and manure them. It is our concern to do these things faithfully, yours to receive them faithfully, and our Lord's to help us in our labor, you in your belief, and all who toil but are conquering the world through him.

I have told you, then, what concerns you. Now I want to tell you what is our own concern. It may seem to some of you that I am bent on telling you something superfluous, and you may be thinking to yourselves, If only he would let us go now! He has already told us what concerns us, but as for what concerns him, what is that to us? I think it is better that we should be of concern to you in our love of each other. You indeed belong to one household now; all of us who are stewards belong to the same household, and we all belong to one Lord. What I give you is not a gift of my own; it is from him, from whom I too receive what I need. If I give you anything of my own, it is bound to be a lie, for when the devil lies, he speaks his own thoughts (John 8:44). And so you must listen to what concerns the steward, whether to congratulate each other, if you find any such among yourselves, or certainly to be instructed in the matter. For how many in this congregation are destined to be stewards? We too once stood where you are standing; we too, who are now seen distributing food to our fellow-servants from a position above them, a few years ago were receiving food with our fellow-servants down where you are. I speak as a bishop to the laity, but how do I know how many future bishops I am speaking to?

The Commands to the Apostles

Let us consider how we are to understand our Lord's commands to those whom he sent to preach the gospel, and let us look at the harvest that was ready for reaping. He said, *You must take with you neither purse, nor bag, nor sandals, and greet no one on the way. And whatever house you go into, you must say: Peace to this house. If there are sons and daughters of peace there, your peace will rest on them, but if not, it will return to you* (Luke 10:4-6). If it rested on others, was it lost? Far be it for the faithful to think so. So even that is not to be taken literally, and therefore neither should we take literally the commands about the purse, the sandals, and the bag, and above all the command to greet no one on the way, for if we accept this command simply, without discussion, it would look as though pride had been forced on us.

Do Not Take a Purse

Let us pay attention to our Lord, who is a true example and help to us. Let us prove that he is a help: *Without me you can do nothing* (John 15:5). Let us prove that he is an example: *Christ suffered for us,* Peter says, *leaving us an example, so that we should follow in his steps* (1 Peter 2:21). Our Lord himself had a purse for his journeys and had entrusted that very purse to Judas. He could even put up with a thief, but because I long to learn from my Lord, I must ask him, Lord, you could put up with a thief, but why did you have something from which he could steal? You have warned me, poor and weak as I am, not to carry a purse, but you yourself carried a purse, and that led you to put up with a thief. If you had not carried a purse, he would have found nothing to steal.

What remains, but that he should say to me, You must understand these words you hear, *You must not carry a purse.* What is a purse? It is something in which money is shut up, something in which wisdom is hidden. What does it mean, *You must not carry a purse*? You must not keep wisdom to yourselves. You must receive the Holy Spirit. There must be a spring within you, not a purse; a giving out, not a shutting up. And the bag means the same as the purse.

Do Not Take Sandals

What are the sandals? The sandals we use are made from the hides of the dead; they are covering for our feet. Therefore, by this we are ordered to renounce dead works. Moses was symbolically warned to do this when the Lord said to him, *Remove the sandals from your feet, for the place where you are standing is holy ground* (Exodus 3:5). What is considered holy ground if not God's Church? So let us stand here and remove our sandals; that is, let us renounce dead works. On the subject of these sandals which we use for walking, the same Lord,

THE HARVEST 89

my Lord himself, consoles me, for if he had not worn sandals, John would not have said of him, *I am not worthy to untie his sandals* (Luke 3:16). So let there be obedience, into which no arrogant severity must be allowed to insinuate itself. I am fulfilling the gospel, you say, because I walk barefoot. You can, but I cannot. Let us take care of what we receive together. How? Let us burn with love, and let us love one another, so that I may love your strength and you may bear with my weakness.

Greet No One on the Way

But what do you think, you who refuse to understand the way these things are said, and are compelled wickedly to slander the Lord himself on the subject of the purse and the sandals? What do you think? Does it really please you that when we are traveling and meet some friends on the way, we should not greet the older ones and not return the greetings of the younger ones? Are you fulfilling the gospel by answering a greeting with silence? In that case you are not behaving like a traveler passing on the way, but rather like a milestone showing the way. So let us give up being stupid, try to understand our Lord's words, and greet no one on the way. For it is not without reason that we are given this command; he would not wish us not to do what he commanded.

What does it mean, then, *Greet no one on the way*? It could indeed be understood simply as an order to obey his commands quickly, so that in saying, *Greet no one on the way,* he means, Ignore everything till you finish what you have been ordered to do, with an exaggeration we often use in conversation. We need not look far for another example. A little later in the same speech he says, *And you, Capernaum, who have been raised to heaven, will be brought down to hell* (Luke 10:15). What does it mean, *you have been raised to heaven*? Does it mean that the walls of that city have touched the clouds or reached the stars? But what does it mean, *you have been raised to heaven*? You think yourself too happy, you are too powerful and too proud. Therefore, just as it was for the sake of emphasis that the city was told, *you have been raised to heaven,* since it was neither raised nor raising itself to heaven, so to emphasize the need for haste we are told, Run, do what I have commanded you, with such speed that no one should delay you on your way even to the smallest degree. In contempt of everything else, hurry to the goal set before you.

Meaning of the Greeting

But there is something else here which is more profound and not so easy to understand, which refers more to me and to all stewards, but also to you who listen to us. When you greet someone, you give greetings to them. Even the ancient

THE HARVEST

writers wrote in their letters, Greetings from one to the other. *Salutatio,* meaning a chance call, is a word derived from *salus,* a greeting. What, then, is meant by, *Greet no one on the way*? Those who greet others on the way greet them by chance. I see you are quick to understand, yet I am obliged to continue, for not all of you have been quick to understand. I heard the voices of those who understood, but there are more whose silence indicates that they need an explanation.

But as we are speaking of a way, let us imagine that we are taking a walk; you who are fast walkers must wait for the slow, and you must walk along together. Well, then, what did I mean by, Those who greet others on the way greet them by chance? They were not on their way to those whom they greet. Where they were going was one thing, but what happened to them by chance on the way was another. Their aim was one thing, but they found their path crossed by another. So what does it mean to greet by chance? To announce salvation by chance. But what is to announce salvation other than to preach the gospel? So if you preach, you must do so with love, not just by chance. Then there are Christians who preach the gospel while seeking nothing but their own interests; about these people the Apostle laments, *For they all seek their own interests, not those of Jesus Christ* (Philippians 2:21). These people were greeting others — that is, announcing salvation, preaching the gospel — but they were seeking something else, and therefore they were greeting by chance. And what does this mean? If you are like this, you act as whoever you are, or rather you do not act as whoever you are, but perhaps you act as someone of that kind does. If you are like this, you do not act, but you are made an instrument for the preaching of the gospel.

Two Kinds of Preachers

The Apostle allowed such people, yet he did not command that there should be such people. They too do something, and something is effected through them. They seek their own ends, but they also preach the word. Pay no attention to what the preacher seeks, but hold fast to what he preaches. His own aims should be no concern of yours. Listen to the greeting that comes from his lips, and hold fast to that greeting. It is not for you to judge his heart. If you see him pursuing other aims, what is that to you? Listen to his greeting, *Do what they tell you to do.* He who said, *Do what they tell you to do,* has made you safe. If their actions are evil, *Do not do what they do* (Matthew 23:3). But if their actions are good, and they greet no one on the way — that is, they do not preach the gospel by chance — then you must follow their example, just as they follow Christ's (1 Corinthians 11:1). If a good man preaches to you, pluck the grape from the vine. If a bad man preaches to you, pluck the grape hanging in the hedge. Such grapes have grown on a vine shoot entangled among thornbushes, and have not sprung from the thorns themselves. To be sure, when you see something like this and are hungry, you must pick carefully, for fear that when you put your hand out to the grapes, the thorns may severely scratch it.

This is what I mean: listen to what is good in such a way that you avoid copying a bad example. Let someone preach by chance and greet you on the way. It will be to his own injury that he refused to listen to Christ's command, *Greet no one on the way*; it will do no injury to you to hold fast to the greeting, whether you hear it from a passerby or from one who comes to greet you purposely. Listen to the Apostle's words on this subject, as I mentioned before. *For what does it matter? Provided that Christ is proclaimed in every way, whether by chance or in truth, and at this I not only rejoice but shall rejoice, for I know that through your prayers it will gain my deliverance* (Philippians 1:18-19).

Peace to this House

Therefore, let Christ's apostles, the preachers of the gospel, be such as this, greeting no one on the way — that is, not seeking or aiming for something different, but announcing the gospel with genuine love — and so let them come to a house and say, *Peace to this house.* They do not say it in words alone; they utter it from the fullness of their hearts. They preach peace and are at peace. They are unlike those of whom it was said, *Peace, peace, but there is no peace* (Jeremiah 8:11).

What does it mean, *Peace, peace, but there is no peace?* They preach it, but are not at peace themselves; they praise it, but do not love it; they say it, but do not practice it. Yet you must receive peace, whether Christ is announced by chance or in truth. Therefore, one who is full of peace and says in greeting, *Peace to this house; if there are sons and daughters of peace there,* his *peace will rest on them: but if not* — for perhaps there are no sons or daughters of peace there, but nothing was lost in the greeting — *it will return to you.* What has not left you will return to you. For this meant, what you announced is of use to you; it was useless to those who refused to receive it. It is not that it was left in vain and therefore you lost your reward. It is returned to you for your desire to give it. It is returned to you for the love with which you gave it, and he will return it to you who made you safe, in the words of the angels, *Peace on earth to people of good will* (Luke 2:14).

CHAPTER 6

INTRODUCTION   In Peter, to whom Jesus entrusted the care of his flock by predicting his martyrdom, Augustine presents the model of a shepherd of souls. Sincere and generous love ought to inspire his action by conquering all egoism, thus giving him the force to face even the sacrifice of his life.

Homilies on John's Gospel 123, 4-5

LOVE AND SACRIFICE

Weakness and Strength of Peter

So when they had eaten, he said to Simon Peter, Simon son of John, do you love me more than these? He answered, Yes, Lord, you know I love you. He said to him, Feed my lambs. And again he asked him, Simon son of John, do you love me? He answered, Yes, Lord, you know I love you. He said to him, Feed my lambs. Then for a third time he asked him, Simon son of John, do you love me? Peter was saddened that he asked him a third time, Do you love me, and told him, Lord, you know all things, you know I love you. He said to him, Feed my sheep. I tell you truly, when you were young you girded yourself and walked where you wished to, but when you are old, you will stretch out your arms, and another will gird you and lead you where you do not wish to go. And he told him this to indicate the death by which he would glorify God (John 21:15-19). He found this death, he who denied and loved, who was raised high by presumption and cast down by denial, who was cleansed by tears, proved by confession, and crowned by suffering. He found this death, to die with perfect love for the name of him, with whom he had promised to die with perverse haste. Strengthened

LOVE AND SACRIFICE

by our Lord's resurrection, he did what in his own weakness he promised prematurely. Christ had to die first for Peter's salvation, then Peter for the proclaiming of Christ. It was the reverse that human rashness had dared to attempt, when truth had arranged this order.

Peter thought (see John 13:37) that he, who was to be set free, would lay down his life for Christ, his deliverer, since it was Christ who had come to lay down his life for all his people, including Peter, which as we see he has already done. Now we may claim the strength of heart to undertake death for our Lord's name — a true strength, since he himself has given it to us — instead of taking a false strength for granted as we do in our own error. Now we need not fear the end of this life, for with our Lord's resurrection the pattern of another life has been shown to us. Now, Peter, you need not fear death, for he lives whose death grieved you, and whose death for us you tried to prevent in your earthly love of him (see Matthew 16:21-22).

You dared to try to forestall your leader and feared his persecutor; but the price has been poured out for you, so now you may follow your redeemer, and follow him completely to death on the cross. You heard his words and have already proved him to be truthful. He, who had foretold that you would deny him, foretold your death.

Feed My Sheep — An Act of Love

Our Lord asks what he knows already — whether Peter loves him — and asks not once but a second and a third time. Each time he hears Peter confess his love for him, and each time he entrusts Peter with the feeding of his sheep. The triple confession repays the triple denial, so that the tongue may not serve love less than fear, and imminent death seems to have evoked a greater response than present life.

Let it be the task of love to feed the Lord's flock, if it is the mark of fear to deny the shepherd. Those who feed Christ's sheep with the intention of making them their own instead of Christ's are proved guilty of loving themselves and not Christ, by a passion for boasting, ruling, or acquiring possessions, instead of a love of obeying, helping, and pleasing God.

It is against those whom the Apostle laments over as seeking their own interests instead of those of Jesus Christ that these words of Christ, so insistently repeated, warn us. For what do the words mean, *Do you love me? Feed my sheep,* other than, If you love me, do not think it is you who feed them, but feed my sheep as mine, not your own. Seek my glory in them, not your own; my rule, not your own; my profit, not your own. This way, you will not be included among those who belong to dangerous times, loving themselves, and the rest that follows from this beginning of evils?

When the Apostle said, *There will be people who love themselves,* he added as a consequence of this, *These will be those who love money, the haughty, the proud, the blasphemous, those who disobey their parents, the ungrateful, the wicked, the impious, those lacking in affection, those who disparage others, the intemperate, the cruel, the unkind, the treacherous, the insolent, the mentally blind, those who love public shows more than they love God, and those who are outwardly devout but whose devotion is meaningless* (2 Timothy 3:2).

Disorders of Self Love

All these evils flow like a fountain from what was placed first — *loving themselves.* Rightly Peter was asked, *Do you love me?* and replied, *Yes, I love you;* and then was told, *Feed my lambs;* and this a second and third time. It is also shown there that the two words for "love" are one and the same in meaning, for even our Lord, when he asked his question for the last time, asked not, *Diligis me,* but, *Amas me?* Therefore, let us love not ourselves but him, and in feeding his sheep seek his interests and not our own, for in some inexplicable way those who love themselves instead of God do not love themselves, and those who love God and not themselves do love themselves. For those who cannot live by their own will indeed die if they love themselves. Therefore, they do not love themselves, when their self-love prevents them from living. But when we love him on whom our lives depend, in not loving ourselves we love ourselves more, because we refrain from loving ourselves in order to love him by whose will we live. So those who feed Christ's sheep must not *love themselves,* nor should they feed the sheep as their own, but as his. They should not desire to seek their own profit from them, like *those who love money,* or rule them, like *the haughty;* or to boast of the honors they get from them, like *the proud;* or to lapse so far as even to create heresies, like *the blasphemous;* nor must they abandon the holy fathers, like *those who disobey their parents;* return evil for good to people who want to correct them because they do not want them to perish, like *the ungrateful;* destroy their own souls and those of others, like *the wicked;* put a sword through the maternal heart of the Church, like *the impious;* fail to have pity on the weak, like *those lacking in affection;* try to disgrace the memory of the saints, like *those who disparage others;* do nothing to restrain their worst passions, like *the intemperate;* quarrel relentlessly, like *the cruel;* refuse to help others, like *the unkind;* tell the enemies of the devout things which they know ought to be kept secret, like *the treacherous;* trouble human modesty by shameless harassment, like *the insolent;* understand nothing of what they are saying or making strong assertions about, like *the mentally blind;* prefer earthly pleasures to spiritual joy, like *those who love public shows more than they love God.*

These vices and others like them, whether all are found in one person or different vices prevail in different people, all in a sense spring from the same root: *self-love.*

Love Conquers Death

The vice which those who feed Christ's sheep have to guard themselves against most of all is seeking their own interests instead of those of Jesus Christ, and using those for whom Christ's blood was shed to further their own ambitions. In those who feed his sheep, the love of Christ should grow to such great spiritual ardor as to conquer even the natural fear of death, which makes us unwilling to die even when we wish to live with Christ. Even the apostle Paul says he longs to depart and be with Christ (Philippians 1:23), yet he laments in deep distress, wishing not to be stripped but rather additionally clothed, so that his mortal body might be absorbed by immortal life (2 Corinthians 5:4-5).

And so our Lord said to the disciple whom he knew loved him, *When you are old, you will stretch out your arms, and another will gird you and lead you where you do not wish to go. And he told him this to indicate the death by which he would glorify God* (John 21:18-19). *You will stretch out your arms,* he says — that is, you will be crucified. But to come to this, *another will gird you and lead you,* not where you wish to go, but *where you do not wish to go.* He told him first what would happen, then how it would happen, for it was not when he had been crucified, but when he was on his way to be crucified, that he was led where he did not wish to go; after his crucifixion he went away, not where he did not wish to go, but rather where he did wish to go. Of course, when he was released from the body he wished to be with Christ, but if it had been possible he would have desired eternal life without the trouble of death, to which trouble he was led unwillingly, but out of which he was led willingly. He went to his death unwillingly, but he willingly conquered it, and so he abandoned that feeling of weakness which makes no one want to die, but which is so natural that not even old age could remove it from blessed Peter, who was told, *When you are old,* you will be led *where you do not wish to go.*

For our consolation, our Savior transformed this feeling even in himself, saying, *Father, if possible, let this cup pass from me* (Matthew 26:39), since he had certainly come to die, was not compelled to die but chose to, and by his own power was to lay down his life and by his own power take it again. But whatever the trouble of death, the power of love must conquer it, the love with which he is loved who, since he is our life, was willing to endure even death for us. If we had no trouble, not even a little, in dying, the glory of the martyrs would not be so great. But if the good shepherd, who laid down his life for his sheep, made so many of those sheep martyrs for himself, how much more must those to whom he entrusts the feeding of his sheep — that

LOVE AND SACRIFICE

is, the teaching and guiding of them — fight to the death for truth and against sin?

Therefore, with the example of his passion set before us, who cannot see that shepherds must rather cling to the shepherd by following his example, if many of the sheep have also followed his example, and under which one shepherd in one flock even the shepherds themselves are sheep? He has indeed made all his sheep, for all of whom he died, for he too was made a sheep, so that he might die for all.

CHAPTER 7

INTRODUCTION   Saint Augustine spoke twice to the people on chapter 24 of the prophet Ezekiel, sermons 46 and 47. The homilies are not exegetical in the strict sense but inspired exhortations from the prophet. The homily is improvised and spontaneous, and thus lacks a cohesiveness so particular to Augustine. It is lengthy and has many digressions. Its beauty lies in the fact that it is a faithful echo of the living word.

Sermon 46

GOD WARNS THE SHEPHERDS

Responsibilities of Shepherds

You have often been taught that all our hope is in Christ and that he is our true glory and our salvation. You are members of the flock of the good shepherd, who watches over Israel and nourishes his people. Yet there are shepherds who want to have the title of shepherd but do not want to fulfill a pastor's duties. Let us recall what God says to his shepherds through the prophet. You must listen attentively; we must listen with fear and trembling.

Thus the word of the Lord came: Son of man, prophesy against the shepherds of Israel, in these words prophesy to them [to shepherds] (Ezekiel 34:1-2). We heard this reading just a moment ago, my brothers, and I have decided to speak to you on this passage. The Lord will help me speak the truth if I do not speak on my own authority, for if I speak on my own authority, I will be a shepherd nourishing myself and not the sheep. However, if my words are the Lord's, then he is nourishing you no matter who speaks. *Thus says the Lord God: Woe to the shepherds of Israel, who have been pasturing themselves! Should not shepherds, rather, pasture sheep?* (Ezekiel 34:2) In other words, true shepherds take care of their sheep, not themselves. This is the principal reason why God condemns those shepherds: they took care of themselves rather than their sheep.

Who are they who nourish themselves? They are the shepherds the Apostle described when he said: *They all seek what is theirs and not what is Christ's* (Philippians 2:21).

I must distinguish carefully between two aspects of the role the Lord has given me, a role that demands rigorous accountability, a role based on the Lord's greatness rather than on my own merit. The first aspect is that I am a Christian; the second, that I am a bishop. I am a Christian for my own sake, whereas I am a bishop for your sake; the fact that I am a Christian is to my own advantage, but I am a leader for your advantage.

Many persons come to God as Christians but not as bishops. Perhaps they travel by an easier road and are less hindered, since they bear a lighter burden. In addition to the fact that I am a Christian and must give God an account of my life, I as a bishop must give him an account of my stewardship as well

Day of Judgment

I put this difficult situation before you so that you may sympathize with me and pray for me. The day will come when all things are brought to judgment. And even if that day is far ahead for the world, as the last day of our own life it is near to each of us. Yet God has wished both — the day on which the world is to end and the day which is to be the end of this life for each of us — to be hidden from us. Do you not fear that unknown day? It must find you prepared when it comes. Since, then, you are given bishops whose duty it is to care for those they lead, and who by no means seek their own advantage through their position as leader but that of those they serve, if any have been set over you whose aim is to rejoice in their leadership, seeking their own honor in it and considering only their own interests, they feed themselves and not their sheep. It is to these that I direct my sermon. You must listen as God's sheep, and see how God has made you safe, no matter who leads you; in other words, whatever I myself am like, he who feeds Israel has given you security. God does not abandon his sheep; the bad shepherds will suffer due punishment and the sheep will receive the promised rewards.

The Shepherds Who Feed Themselves

Let us consider the unflattering words of God which Scripture addresses to shepherds who feed

GOD WARNS THE SHEPHERDS

themselves and not the sheep: *You have fed off their milk, worn their wool, and slaughter the fatlings, but the sheep you have not pastured. You did not strengthen the weak nor heal the sick nor bind up the injured. You did not bring back the strayed, nor seek the lost, but you lorded it over them harshly and brutally. So they were scattered for lack of a shepherd* (Ezekiel 34:3-5).

This is spoken to the shepherds who feed themselves and not the sheep; it speaks of their concern and their neglect. What is their concern? *You have fed off their milk, and worn their wool.* And so the Apostle asks: *Who plants a vineyard and does not eat of its yield? What shepherd does not nourish himself with the milk of his flock?* (1 Corinthians 9:7) Thus, we learn that the milk of the flock is whatever temporal support and sustenance God's people give to those who are placed over them. It is of this that the Apostle was speaking in the passage just quoted.

The Selflessness of Paul

Although he chose to support himself by the labor of his own hands and did not ask for milk from the sheep, the Apostle did say that he had the right to receive the milk, for the Lord had established that they who preach the gospel should live by the gospel (1 Corinthians 9:14). Paul also says that other fellow apostles made use of this right, a right granted them, and not unlawfully usurped. But Paul went further by not taking what was rightfully his. He forgave the debt, whereas the others did not demand what was not due them. Therefore, Paul went further. Perhaps his action was foreshadowed by the Good Samaritan, who, when he brought the sick man to the inn, said: *If you spend any more, I will repay you on my way back* (Luke 10:35).

What more can I say concerning those shepherds who do not need the milk of the flock? They are more merciful, or rather, they carry out a more abundant ministry of mercy. They are able to do so, and they do it. Let them receive praise, but do not condemn the others. The Apostle himself did not seek what was given. However, he wanted the sheep to be fruitful, not sterile and unable to give milk.

Paul's Example

Once, when Paul was in great need, in chains for his confession of the truth, his fellow Christians sent him what was necessary for his wants and needs. He thanked them with these words: *You have done well to share in my need. It is true that I have learned to be self-sufficient in whatever circumstances I find myself. I know what it is to have plenty, and I have learned how to endure privation. I can do all things in him who strengthens me. Still, you have done well to send things for my use* (Philippians 4:11-14).

Just as this indicates in what sense they had done well, it also shows what Paul himself sought, namely, to avoid being numbered among those who feed themselves and not the sheep. Paul does not rejoice so much in his own deliverance from need as he does in their generosity. What, then, was he seeking? *I do not set my heart upon gifts,* he says; *all I seek is the fruit of my labor* (Philippians 4:17). Not that I may be filled, he says, but that you may not remain empty.

Duties of the Faithful

As for those who cannot support themselves with their own hands as Paul did, let them take from the milk of the sheep, let them receive what is necessary for their needs, but do not let them neglect the weakness of the sheep. Do not let them seek any benefit for themselves, lest they appear to be preaching the gospel for the sake of their own need and privation; rather, let them provide the light of the true word for the sake of the enlightenment of all, for they are like lamps. It has been said, *Let your belts be fastened and your lamps burning,* and, *No one lights a lamp and puts it under a bushel basket; rather, he puts it on a lampstand, that it may give light to all who are in the house. So let your light shine before all in order that they may see your good works and glorify your Father who is in heaven* (Matthew 5:15-16)

Now if a lamp has been lighted for you in your house, would you not add oil to keep it from going out? On the other hand, if the lamp received the oil and failed to shine, it was obviously not fit to be put on the lampstand and should have been discarded at once.

Whatever is indispensable for living must be accepted; it is charity to offer it. Only let not the gospel be for sale, with preachers demanding a price for it and making their living from it. If they sell it like that, they are selling for a pittance something that is of great value. Let them receive support in their need from the people, but payment for their stewardship from the Lord. No, it is not right for the people to give payment to those who serve them out of love of the gospel. Payment is to be expected only from the one who also grants salvation.

Why, then, are they rebuked? Why are they accused? Because when they took the milk and covered themselves with the wool, they neglected the sheep. They sought only to serve their own cause and not Christ's.

The Example of Paul

I have explained what it means to have fed off their milk. Now let us consider what it means to wear their wool. One who gives milk gives sustenance, while one who gives wool gives honor. These are precisely the two things that pastors who feed themselves and not the sheep look for from the people — the benefit of having their wants supplied as well as the favor of honor and praise.

Yes, clothing can well be taken to mean honor, since it covers nakedness. Every man, without exception, is weak. And who is the person placed over you except someone just like yourself? Your pastor is in the flesh; he is mortal. He eats, sleeps, and awakens. He was born and he is going to die. When you think about it, he is, in himself, simply a man. But it is true that you make him something more by giving him honor; it is as if you were covering what is weak.

Consider the nature of the clothing that the apostle Paul received from God's good people. He said: *You have received me like an angel of God. I testify that if it were possible you would have torn out your eyes and given them to me* (Galatians 4:14-15). Indeed, great honor was shown him. But did he then spare sinners because of that honor, perhaps out of fear that it would be refused and that he would receive less praise when he gave blame? Had he done so, he would be among those shepherds who feed themselves and not the sheep. He would then say to himself: "What has this to do with me? Let everyone do what he will; my sustenance is safe, and my honor too. I have enough milk and wool, so let each one do as he likes." But then are things really secure for you if each one does as he pleases? I want to make you not a leader over the people, but one of the people themselves, for *if one member suffers, all the members suffer with him* (1 Corinthians 12:26).

In recalling how they treated him, the Apostle does not want to appear forgetful of the honor they did him. Therefore, he gives testimony that they received him like an angel of God, that if it were possible, they would be willing to tear out their eyes and give them to him. Yet he still comes to the sheep that is ill, to the one that is diseased, to cut the wound and not to spare the diseased part. He says: *Have I then become your enemy by preaching the truth?* (Galatians 4:16) He has fed off the milk of the sheep, as I mentioned a short time ago, and he has worn their wool, but he did not neglect his sheep. He did not seek what was his but what was Christ's.

Serving the Wayward

Far be it for me, then, to tell you: "Live as you like; you are bound to be safe. God will destroy no one; all you have to do is to hold the Christian faith. He will not destroy what he has redeemed; he will not destroy those for whom he shed his blood. If you want to amuse yourselves at the theater, go and do so. What harm is there? And those feasts too, which are celebrated throughout the city, at which a joyful crowd feasts together at the public table, thinking themselves happy when they are really destroying themselves — go and join them without fear. God's mercy is great enough to forgive us everything. Crown yourselves with roses before they begin to fade. Feast together in the house of your God when you want to. Fill yourselves with food and wine in the company of your own people, for this created substance was given for you to enjoy to the fullest; for God did not give it to pagans and wicked people and not give it to you." If I were to say this, perhaps I would attract a greater crowd. And though there might be some who think me wrong to say it, I would offend but a few and win over a multitude. If I were to do this, speaking not the words of God, not the words of Christ, but my own, I would be a shepherd feeding myself and not my sheep.

Be an Example for the Faithful

After the Lord had shown what wicked shepherds esteem, he spoke about what they neglect. The defects of the sheep are widespread. There are very few healthy and sound sheep, few that are solidly sustained by the food of truth, and few that enjoy the good pasture that God gives them. But the wicked shepherds do not spare such sheep. It is not enough that they neglect those that are ill and weak, those that go astray and are lost. They even try, as far as it is in their power, to kill the strong and healthy. Yet such sheep live; yes, by God's mercy they live. As for the wicked shepherds themselves, they kill the sheep. "How do they kill them?" you ask. By their wicked lives and by giving bad example. Or was God's servant, who was high among the members of the chief shepherd, told this in vain: *Show yourself as an example of good works toward all* (Titus 2:7), and, *Be an example to the faithful* (1 Timothy 4:12)?

Even the strong sheep, turning their eyes from the Lord's laws and looking at the man set over them, notice when their shepherd is living wickedly and begin to wonder in their hearts: "If my pastor lives like that, why should I not live like him?" The wicked shepherd kills the strong sheep. But if he kills the strong one, what does he do to the rest? After all, by his wicked life he kills even the sheep he had not strengthened but had found strong and hardy.

I appeal to your love, and again I say, even if the sheep have life and if they are strong in the word of the Lord, and if they hold fast to what they have heard from their Lord, *Do what they say but not what they do* (Matthew 23:3), still, as far as he himself is concerned, the shepherd who lives a wicked life before the people kills the sheep under his care. Let such a shepherd not deceive himself just because the sheep is not dead, for though it still lives, he is a murderer. It is like when the lustful man looks on a woman with desire. She remains chaste, but he has committed adultery. The Lord said in plain truth: *Whoever has looked upon a woman with desire has already committed adultery with her in his heart* (Matthew 5:28); he has not entered her bedroom, yet he has ravished her within the bedroom of his heart.

GOD WARNS THE SHEPHERDS

Therefore, anyone who lives wickedly before those who have been placed under his care kills, as far as he himself is concerned, even the strong. Whoever imitates him, dies; whoever does not, has life. But as for he himself, he kills both of them. *You slaughtered the fatlings but the sheep you have not pastured* (Ezekiel 34:3).

Prepare Your Soul for Temptation

You have already been told about the wicked things that shepherds desire. Let us now consider what they neglect. *You did not strengthen the weak nor heal the sick nor bind up the injured,* that is, what was broken. *You did not bring back the strayed, nor seek the lost. What was strong you have destroyed* (Ezekiel 34:3-4). Yes, you have cut it down and killed it. The sheep is weak — that is to say, its heart is weak — and so, incautious and unprepared, it may give in to temptations.

The negligent shepherd fails to say to the believer, *My son, come to the service of God, stand fast in fear and in righteousness, and prepare your soul for temptation* (Sirach 2:1). A shepherd who does say this strengthens the one who is weak and makes him strong. Such a believer will then not hope for the prosperity of this world. But if he has been taught to hope for worldly gain, he will be corrupted by prosperity. When adversity comes, he will be wounded and perhaps destroyed.

The builder who builds in such a manner is not building the believer on rock but upon sand. *But the rock was Christ* (1 Corinthians 10:4). Christians must imitate Christ's sufferings, not set their hearts on pleasures. He who is weak will be strengthened when told: "Yes, expect the temptations of this world, but the Lord will deliver you from them all if your heart has not abandoned him, for it was to strengthen your heart that he came to suffer and die, came to be spit upon and crowned with thorns, came to be accused of shameful things, and yes, came to be fastened to the wood of the cross. All these things he did for you, and you did nothing. He did them not for himself, but for you."

Suffering with Christ

But what sort of shepherds are they who, for fear of giving offense, not only fail to prepare the sheep for the temptations that threaten them, but even promise them worldly happiness? God himself made no such promise to this world. On the contrary, God foretold hardship upon hardship in this world until the end of time. And you claim that the Christian is exempt from these troubles? Precisely because he is a Christian, he is destined to suffer more in this world.

The Apostle says: *All who desire to live a holy life in Christ will suffer persecution* (2 Timothy 3:12). But you, shepherd, seek what is yours and not what is

GOD WARNS THE SHEPHERDS

Christ's; you disregard what the Apostle says: *All who want to live a holy life in Christ will suffer persecution.* You say instead: "If you live a holy life in Christ, all good things will be yours in abundance. If you do not have children, you will embrace and nourish all people, and none of them shall die." Is this the way you build up the believer? Take note of what you are doing and where you are placing him. You have built him on sand. The rains will come, the river will overflow and rush in, the winds will blow, and the elements will dash against that house of yours. It will fall, and its ruin will be great.

Lift him up from the sand and put him on the rock. Let him be in Christ, if you wish him to be a Christian. Let him turn his thoughts to sufferings, however unworthy they may be in comparison to Christ's. Let him center his attention on Christ, who was without sin and yet made restitution for what he had not done. Let him consider Scripture, which says to him: *He chastises every son whom he acknowledges* (Hebrews 12:6). Let him prepare to be chastised, or else not seek to be acknowledged as a son.

Scripture says, *God chastises every son whom he acknowledges.* But the bad shepherd says, "Perhaps I will be exempt." If he is exempt from the suffering of his chastisements, then he is not numbered among God's sons. You will ask: "Does God indeed punish every son?" Yes, every one, just as he chastised his only Son. His only Son, born of the substance of the Father, equal to the Father *in the form of God* (Philippians 2:6), the Word through whom all things were made, could not be chastised. For this reason he was clothed with flesh so that he might know chastisement. God punishes his only Son, who is without sin; does he then leave unpunished an adopted son who is with sin? The Apostle says that we have been called to adoption. We have been adopted as sons, that we might be coheirs with the only Son, and also that we might be his inheritance: *Ask of me and I will give you the nations as your inheritance* (Psalm 2:8). Christ gave us the example by his own sufferings.

CHAPTER 8

INTRODUCTION Commenting on the parable of the talents (Matthew 25:14-30), Augustine explains that it is the duty of the bishop to dispense to others and to spread the word of the Lord. His recompense is the salvation of the faithful.

But the heads of families have an task analogous to that of the bishop: to watch that evil does not penetrate the family community.

Sermon 94

THE BISHOP'S COLLABORATORS

The Prophet On Expenditure

Certainly my reverend brothers and fellow bishops have thought fit to visit and gladden us with their presence, but for some reason they are unwilling to help me in my weariness. I have told you this in their own hearing, in the hope that your hearing it may somehow intercede with them on my behalf, so that when I ask them, they too may give you a sermon. May they use the talents they have received, and think fit to work rather than make excuses. But from me, worn out as I am and hardly able to speak, willingly hear these few words. For we also have a booklet due to be read to us on the blessings God has given through the holy martyr [Stephen]; may we listen to that more willingly together. What is our subject, then? What shall I say to you? You have heard described in the gospel both the merit of the good servants and the punishment of the bad.

The whole wickedness of that servant who was reproved and severely condemned was this: that he refused to make use of the talent he had been given. He kept what he had received intact, but his

THE BISHOP'S COLLABORATORS 123

master wanted profit. God is greedy for our salvation. If a servant is thus condemned for not having used his master's money, what must be the fear of those who lose his money? Therefore, we ourselves are stewards; it is we who pay out and you who receive. The profit we want is that you should live good lives.

That is the profit that we make on our expenditure. But do not think that such expenditure is not also your own concern. Though you cannot distribute money from this superior position, you can do so wherever you are. Where Christ is censured, you must defend him; answer the grumblers, reprove the blasphemers, and avoid their company. Thus, you make good use of your money if there are some people you can show as your profit. Act my part in your own homes. A bishop is so called because he superintends, because he cares for people by watching over them. Everyone, then, who is the head of his household must exercise the office of bishop in his own home and watch over the faith of his own people so that none of them falls into heresy, neither his wife, nor his son, nor his daughter, nor even his servant, for whom so great a price was paid. The Apostle's teaching has placed the master above the servant, and the servant below the master (Ephesians 6:5; Titus 2:9). Yet Christ has paid a single price for both. You must not despise the least of your own people, but attend to the salvation of the members of your household with all care. If you do this, you use your money well. You will not be lazy servants, nor will you fear a condemnation so much to be loathed.

CHAPTER 9

INTRODUCTION   *The Johannine allegory of the Good Shepherd (John 10:1-16) is at the center of this sermon which is a meditation of the bishop on his own responsibilities, a severe warning to clergy who seek themselves rather than Christ, and an exhortation and encouragement to the faithful to respond to the zeal of true shepherds. The faithful are advised to gather from the hirelings the good they say and not be swayed from the good by their bad example.*

Sermon 137

SHEPHERDS AND HIRELINGS

Christ Is the Head of the Church

You are not ignorant believers, my dear friends, and so I know that because your Master in heaven, in whom you have put your hope, has taught you, you have learnt that our Lord Jesus Christ, who has already suffered for us and risen again, is the head of the Church, and the Church is his body, and its health, as it were, exists in the unity of the members in his body and the bond of love which unites them.

Anyone whose love has become cold is sick in the body of Christ. But he, who has already exalted our head, has also the power to heal our sick members as long as they are not cut off by excessive wickedness and cling to the body until they are healed. Any member which still clings to the body has the hope of recovery, but one which has been cut off can neither be healed nor restored. Since, then, he is the head of the Church, and the Church is his body, the whole Christ is both head and body. He has already risen from the dead. Therefore, our head is in heaven. Our head intercedes for us. Our head, who is sinless and immortal, now propitiates God for our sins, so that we too at last, rising again and transfigured in heavenly glory, may follow our head, for where the head is, there too are the rest of the members. But while we are here on earth, we are his members; we must not despair, for we are to follow our head.

Christ Suffers in His Mystical Members

Consider, my friends, the love of our head himself. Although he is already in heaven, he still suffers on earth as long as the Church suffers here. Here Christ is hungry, thirsty, poor, lonely, sick, and imprisoned. He has told us that he suffers whatever his own body suffers here on earth; on the last day, when he separates his own body and places it on the right, and places the rest, all those who despise him, on the left, he will say to those on the right: *Come, you whom my Father has blessed, receive the kingdom which has been ready for you since the beginning of the world* (Matthew 25:34).

What have they done to deserve this? *For I was hungry, and you gave me food* (Matthew 25:35); and so his narration continues, as if it were he himself who had received their kindly attentions, till at last they ask in bewilderment, *Lord, when did we see you hungry, a stranger, and in prison?* (Matthew 25:39) And he tells them: *Whatever you did for the least of my people, you did for me* (Matthew 25:40). Thus, even in our own bodies, our heads are above and our feet on the ground. Yet when someone treads on your foot in a crowd, is it not your head which says, You are treading on me? No one has trodden on your head, nor on your tongue. Your head is above, in safety; nothing has harmed it. Yet, because of the bond of love which unites our bodies from head to foot, the tongue did not keep aloof from the foot, but said, You are treading on me, although no one had touched it.

Thus, as the tongue, which no one has touched, says, You are treading on me, so Christ the head, whom no one treads on, says, *I was hungry, and you gave me food.* And to those who failed to do this, he says, *I was hungry, but you gave me nothing to eat.* And how did he conclude? Thus: *They will go to eternal fire, but the righteous to eternal life* (Matthew 25:46).

Peter, Do You Love Me? Lord, I Love You.

So when our Lord spoke just now, he said he was the shepherd, and he said he was also the door. You have both here: *I am the door,* and *I am the shepherd.* He is the door as head, and the shepherd as body. For he asked Peter, on whom alone he formed his Church, *Peter, do you love me?* Peter answered, *Yes, Lord, I love you. Feed my sheep.* And he asked a third time: *Peter, do you love me?* Peter was saddened because he asked him for a third time (John 21:15-17). It was as if he who saw the bad conscience of the disciple who had denied him could not see the

SHEPHERDS AND HIRELINGS

faith of the same disciple who had confessed his belief in him.

But Jesus did know him; he knew him even when Peter did not know himself. For example, he did not know himself when he said: *I shall be with you to death* (Luke 22:33ff), nor did he know how ill he was. As indeed usually happens in the case of those who are ill, the sick do not know what is the matter with them, but the physician knows, even though the sick actually suffer the illness and the physician does not. The physician is better at telling what is happening to the sick than the sick themselves.

So at that time Peter was sick, but our Lord was his physician. Peter declared that he was strong, though he was not, but our Lord felt his pulse and told him he would deny him three times. And so it turned out as the physician foretold instead of as the sick man presumed (Luke 22:55ff). Therefore, after his resurrection our Lord questioned Peter, not because he did not know with what feeling Peter would confess his love for Christ, but to blot out Peter's triple denial of fear with his triple confession of love.

Imitate the Humility of Christ

So our Lord asks Peter, *Peter, do you love me?* (John 21:15) as if he were asking, What will you give me, what will you offer me, because you love me? What was Peter to offer the Lord who rose again, ascended to heaven, and sat at the right hand of the Father? It is as if he were saying, This is what you will give me, what you will offer me, if you love me: you will feed my sheep. You must enter by the door, not climb in by another way. You were told this when the gospel (John 10:1ff) was read to you: *He who enters by the door is the shepherd, but he who climbs in by another way is a thief and robber; he seeks to rout, scatter, and destroy.*

Who is it who enters by the door? One who enters through Christ. Who is such a person? One who imitates Christ's passion, who acknowledges Christ's humility, so that, since God was made human for us, we must acknowledge that we are not God but human. Those humans who wish to appear to be God do not imitate him who, though he was God, was made human. You are not told to be something less than you are, but to acknowledge what you are. Acknowledge yourself to be sick, human, a sinful; acknowledge that he justifies, and that you yourself are polluted.

Let the pollution of your heart appear in your confession, and then you will belong to Christ's flock, for the confession of your sins calls the physician who will heal you, just as the sick who declare they are healthy do not ask for the physician. Surely you remember the Pharisee and the tax collector who went up to the temple? One boasted of his health; the other showed his wounds to the

SHEPHERDS AND HIRELINGS

physician. The Pharisee said: *God, I thank you that I am not like this tax collector* (Luke 18:10ff). He boasted of his superiority over the other. So if the tax collector had been a healthy man, the Pharisee would have envied him; for there would have been nothing to raise him above the other. In what state, then, was this man, who would have envied the other, when he came to the temple? He was by no means healthy, but since he declared he was, it was not he who came down from the temple healed.

Meanwhile, the other, with eyes cast to the ground, not daring to lift them to heaven, beat his breast and said: *God be merciful to me, a sinner.* And what was our Lord's comment? *Truly I tell you, it was the tax collector rather than the Pharisee who came down from the temple justified, for all who exalt themselves will be humbled, but those who humble themselves will be exalted* (Luke 18:13ff). So those who exalt themselves want to climb into the sheepfold by another way, but those who humble themselves enter the sheepfold by the door. That is why he said of one, *he enters,* but of the other, *he climbs.* You see, one who climbs, one who seeks the heights, does not enter, but falls. On the other hand, one who humbles himself so as to enter by the door does not fall, but is the shepherd.

CHAPTER 9

Two Ways of Preaching the Gospel

There are three persons our Lord told us about, and so we must examine them as they appear in the gospel (John 10:1ff): the shepherd, the hireling, and the thief. When the gospel was read to you, I presume you noticed how our Lord described the three. The shepherd he described as laying down his life for the sheep and entering by the door. The thief and robber, he said, climb in by another way. The hireling, he told us, runs away at the sight of the wolf or even the thief because he does not care about the sheep, for he is a hireling, not the shepherd.

One enters by the door, because he is the shepherd; another climbs in by another way, because he is a thief; and the last takes fright and runs away when he sees those who are bent on carrying off the sheep, because he is a hireling and does not care about the sheep. If we have understood the nature of these three characters, then you yourselves understand whom you must love, whom you must tolerate, and of whom you have to beware.

You are to love the shepherd, tolerate the hireling, and beware of the robber. There are people in the Church, as the Apostle tells us (Philippians 1:21), who preach the gospel as opportunity occurs, seeking from others their own advantage, whether in the form of pecuniary reward, honors, or human praise. They preach the gospel with the desire to receive a reward of whatever sort, seeking not so much the salvation of those to whom they preach as their own advantage. But those who hear salvation from the lips of one who is without salvation must believe in him of whom he preaches, but not place their hope in him through whom salvation is preached to them. So it is the preacher who will suffer loss, and those to whom he preaches will be the ones to gain.

The Church of the Jews and Gentiles

There is a saying of our Lord about the Pharisees, *They sit in the chair of Moses* (Matthew 23:2ff). Our Lord did not mean the Pharisees alone, but it is as if he sent those who believed in Christ to the Jewish school, to learn there the way to the kingdom of heaven. Did our Lord not come to establish the Church, and to separate even the Jews of right faith, hope, and love like grain from chaff, to make one wall of the circumcised, to which another wall of the uncircumcised, the Gentiles, was to be joined, for which two walls coming from opposite directions he himself would be the cornerstone (see Romans 9:30-33; Ephesians 2:14-16)?

Was it not the same Lord, then, who said of these two peoples who were to become one, *I have other sheep, too, who are not of this fold*? But in this case he was speaking to the Jews, and added, *I must bring these also to make one flock, with one shepherd* (John

10:16). Therefore, there were two boats from which he had called his disciples. They signified two peoples, when the disciples let down their nets and raised them with such a large catch that the nets almost broke: *And they loaded two boats* (Luke 5:2ff), as the gospel says. The two boats signified one Church, but formed of two peoples, the Church that was joined in Christ, though coming from opposite directions. The same meaning is also to be found in the two wives, Leah and Rachel (Genesis 29:9), who had one husband, Jacob. And meaning the same two peoples, there are also the two blind men sitting by the wayside whose eyes our Lord opened (Matthew 10:30).

And if you pay attention to the Scriptures, you will find the two Churches, which are not two but one, signified in many places. The cornerstone is able to make one people out of two. The shepherd is able to make one flock out of two. Therefore, since our Lord will teach the Church and have his own school contrary to that of the Jews, as we now see, was he likely to send those who believed in him to the Jews for teaching? Under the names of Pharisees and Scribes he signified those people who would be found in his Church, who would say one thing and do another, but in the person of Moses he symbolized himself. And indeed Moses acted the part of our Lord, and therefore used to veil his face when he spoke to the people (Exodus 34:34). As long as those within the law were given up to worldly joys and pleasures and sought an

SHEPHERDS AND HIRELINGS

earthly kingdom, their faces were veiled to prevent them from seeing Christ in the Scriptures, and when the veil was removed, after our Lord's passion, the secrets of the temple were seen from top to bottom (Matthew 27:51), and the apostle Paul says clearly, *But when you have turned to Christ, the veil will be removed* (2 Corinthians 3:16ff). But those who have not turned to Christ, even though they read Moses, have veiled hearts as the Apostle says. So when our Lord prefigured the people of that kind who would be found in his Church, what did he say? *The Scribes and Pharisees sit in the chair of Moses: do what they tell you to, but not what they do* (Matthew 23:2ff).

Do What They Tell You to, But Not What They Do

When bad priests hear those words, which are directed against themselves, they wish to pervert them. In fact, I have heard some wish to pervert this saying. Would they not, if they were allowed to, blot it out from the gospel? But because they cannot blot it out, they seek to pervert it. But God's ever-present grace and mercy prevent them from doing so, for he has fenced all his sayings with his own truth and kept them in their place, so that whoever wants to cut something off them or introduce something by reading the words wrongly or misinterpreting them, the intelligent person may join what has been cut off from Scripture to Scripture, and read the complete text, and so will discover the meaning which the other wanted to misinterpret. What, then, do you think they say about them of whom it is written, *Do what they tell you to?*

The words are indeed addressed to lay people. So when the laity who want to lead good lives pay attention to a bad priest, what do they say to themselves? Our Lord said: *Do what they tell you to, but not what they do.* We must walk in the way of our Lord, not follow this man's example. We must hear from him the words that are not his own, but God's. We must follow God; let this man follow his own desires, for if we tried to defend ourselves before God using the argument, Lord, we saw your own priest living badly and so we did the same, would he not answer us, You worthless servants, have you not heard my words, *Do what they tell you to, but not what they do?*

But as for the laity who are bad and unfaithful, who do not belong to Christ's flock or to Christ's grain which is tolerated like chaff on the threshing floor, what do they say to themselves when God's word censures them? Go away; why speak to us? If not even bishops and priests do what you tell them to do, the why are you compelling us to do so? They are not seeking an advocate for themselves in a bad cause, but a companion in punishment; however, he, whoever he is, whose bad example they followed, will never defend them on the day of judgment. Just as the devil seduces people, not to reign with them but to be condemned with them, so do all

SHEPHERDS AND HIRELINGS

who follow the bad seek companions for themselves on the way to hell, rather than a defense to lead them to the kingdom of heaven.

Empty Excuses of Bad Pastors

How, then, do they pervert this saying when those who lead bad lives are told, Our Lord has rightly said, *Do what they tell you to, but not what they do*? They agree it is rightly said; for you are commanded, they say, to do what we tell you to, but not what we do. We offer sacrifice, but you are not allowed to do so. You see the cunning of such people, whom I can only call hirelings, for if they were shepherds, they would not speak in such a way. Therefore, to shut their mouths, our Lord continued, *They sit in the chair of Moses; do what they tell you to, but not what they do, for they say one thing and do another.*

What does this mean, then, my friends? If he were speaking about the offering of sacrifice, would he have said, *For they say one thing and do another*? For they perform the sacrifice, they make the offering to God. What is the difference between their words and actions? Listen to what follows: *For they tie unbearably heavy burdens and place them on the necks of people, burdens which they themselves would not touch with one finger* (Matthew 23:4ff). He clearly blamed them for this, as his description indicates.

But when they seek to pervert this saying in the way that they do, they show that they seek nothing but their own interests in the Church; nor they have not even read the gospel, for if they knew that page and had read the whole passage, they would never dare say what they say.

Scribes and Pharisees in the Church

But you must pay closer attention, for there are such people in the Church. Let no one tell us, He spoke only about Pharisees, Scribes, and Jews, for there are no such people as this in the Church. Who, then, are all those of whom our Lord says, *Not all who say to me, Lord, Lord, will enter the kingdom of heaven* (Matthew 7:21-23)? And he added, *On that day many will say to me, Lord, Lord, have we not prophesied in your name, in your name performed many miracles, and in your name eaten and drunk?* Is it the Jews who do these things in the name of Christ? It is certainly clear that he is speaking of Christians. But what follows? *Then I shall tell them: I have never known you. Go away from me, all you who do evil.* Listen to the Apostle (Philippians 1:17) sighing over such people. He says that some preach the gospel for love, others for opportunity, about whom he says, *They do not preach the gospel rightly.* The matter is right, but they themselves are wrong. What they preach is right, but the preachers are wrong. Why are they wrong? Because they seek

SHEPHERDS AND HIRELINGS

something else in the Church; they are not seeking God. If they sought God, they would be chaste, for God is the soul's legitimate husband. Whoever seeks something from God other than God does not seek God chastely.

You see, my friends, if a wife loves her husband because he is wealthy, then she is not chaste, for rather than loving her husband, she loves his money. If she truly loves her husband, she will love him even when he is poor, even when he has nothing. But if she loves him because of his wealth, what happens if (such are the chances of human life) his property is confiscated and he suddenly finds himself destitute? Perhaps she will renounce him because what she loved was not her husband but his possessions. But if she truly loves her husband, she loves him even more as a poor man, for she loves with compassion.

Seek God Alone

And yet, my friends, our God can never be poor. He is rich, he has made all things, heaven and earth, the sea and the angels. Whatever we can see in the heavens and whatever is beyond our sight he has created. Even so, it is none of these treasures that we must love, but their creator, for all he has promised you is himself. Find something more precious, and he will give it to you. The earth, the sky, and the angels are glorious things, but even more glorious is he who has created them. So those who preach God because they love God, those who preach God because of God, feed his sheep, and are not hirelings. It was the chastity of the soul that our Lord Jesus Christ demanded when he asked Peter, *Peter, do you love me?* What does it mean, *Do you love me* (John 21:15)? Are you chaste? Have you a heart that is not adulterous? Do you seek in the Church, not your own interests, but mine? If, then, you are such a person and you love me, *feed my sheep.* You will not be a hireling, but a shepherd.

Shepherds and Hirelings

So those over whom the Apostle sighs were not preaching chastely. But does he say *What does it matter so long as Christ is preached in every way, whether in pretense or truth* (Philippians 1:18)? So he allowed the presence of hirelings. The shepherd preaches Christ in truth; the hireling preaches Christ in pretense, seeking some other end. Yet both preach Christ. Listen to the words of the shepherd Paul: *Let Christ be preached, whether in pretense or in truth.*

Even the shepherd wanted to keep the hireling, for they do what they can; they are as useful as they are capable of being. But when he looked for someone with other needs in view, someone whose ways the weak could imitate, he says: *I have sent you Timothy, to remind you of my ways* (1 Corinthians

4:17). And what does he mean? I have sent you a shepherd to remind you of my ways; in other words, I have sent you someone who walks in the same way as I do. And in sending a shepherd, what does he say? *I have no one who is so much of my own mind, one who cares about you with sincere affection* (Philippians 2:20-21). Were there not many with him? But what follows? *For all who seek their own interests, not those of Jesus Christ.* In other words, I wanted to send you a shepherd, for there are many hirelings, but it would not have been right to send a hireling. A hireling is sent for other purposes and to carry out other tasks, but for Paul's purpose at that time, a shepherd was essential. And he could hardly find one shepherd among all the hirelings, for there were few shepherds but many hirelings. But what is said about the hirelings? *I tell you truly, they have received their reward* (Matthew 6:2). But what does the Apostle say about the shepherd? *But those who cleanse themselves from such things will be utensils sanctified for honor, useful to the Lord, always ready for every good work* (2 Timothy 2:21) — not prepared for some things and unprepared for others, but *ready for every good work.* This is what he said about shepherds.

The Flight of the Hirelings

But now we shall talk about the hirelings. *When a hireling sees a wolf lying in wait for the sheep, he takes flight.* That is what our Lord said. Why does he do this? *Because he does not care about the sheep* (John 11:13). So the hireling is useful as long as he sees no wolf and no thief or robber; when he sees any of these, he takes flight. And what hireling is there who does not take flight from the Church, when he sees a wolf or robber? Wolves and robbers abound. It is they who climb in by another way. Who are these climbers? The Donatists who want to plunder Christ's sheep, they are the ones who climb in by another way. They do not enter through Christ, for they are not humble. They climb because of their pride. What does it mean, they climb? They are raised high. Where do they climb from? By another way — the way by which they want to be known. Those who are not in unity are of another way, and climb by that way — that is, they are raised high and want to carry off the sheep. Observe how they climb. We, they say, sanctify, justify, and make people righteous. That is the height to which they have climbed. But *those who exalt themselves will be humbled* (Luke 14:11). Our Lord God is able to humble them.

The wolf, on the other hand, is the devil. He lies in wait to deceive, and so do those who follow him, for it is said that they indeed wear the skins of sheep but are inwardly rapacious wolves (Matthew 7:15). If a hireling sees people saying evil things, or believing in them to the destruction of their souls, or doing something wicked or offensive, and yet because they seem to be people of some importance in the Church, and if he hopes for advantage from them — he is a hireling. And so when he sees people perishing in sin, when he sees the wolf following them, seizing them by the throat and dragging them off to eternal punishment, he does not say to them, What are you doing is sinful; he does not reprove them, for fear of losing his own advantage. So this is what is meant by, *When he sees a wolf he takes flight:* he refrains from telling the people that what they are doing is wrong. This is the flight not of the body but of the soul. One whom you see standing firm in body takes flight in spirit, when he sees people falling into sin and fails to tell them about it, even when they are assembled together.

Bunches of Grapes in the Thorns

My friends, do you think that a priest or bishop does not sometimes climb, and from his superior position does not say something other than forbidding you to rob others of their possessions, to cheat people or commit crimes? Those who sit in the chair of Moses can say nothing other than that, and so it is the chair that speaks through them, not they themselves. Then what is meant by, *Are grapes gathered from thornbushes, or figs from thistles?* (Matthew 5:16) and *Every tree is known by its fruit* (Matthew 5:20)? Can a Pharisee speak anything good? The Pharisee is a thornbush. How can I pick grapes from a thornbush? You yourself, Lord, have told me: *Do what they tell you to, but not what they do* (Matthew 23:3). You tell me to pluck grapes from thornbushes, though you asked, *Are grapes gathered from thornbushes?* You answer me: I did not tell you to pick grapes from thornbushes, but pay proper attention and see if, as often happens, a vine branch as it winds along the ground has not become entangled in a thornbush. For sometimes we come upon that, my friends, because there is a thornbush hedge where the vine is planted in reed grass, and the vine shoots grow into the hedge, so that bunches of grapes hang among the thorns. Anyone seeing them plucks them, yet not from the thornbush, but from the vine which is enclosed in it. So it is thus that the Pharisees are thornbushes, but where they sit in Moses' chair the vine has enveloped them, and bunches of grapes — that is, good words and good precepts — hang on them. You are to pick the grapes, but do not let the thorns prick you when you pick them. *Do what they tell you to, but not what they do.* They only prick you if you do what they do. Therefore, to pick the grapes without getting caught on the thorns, *Do what they tell you to, but not what they do.* Their acts are thorns and their words are grapes, but they are grapes from the vine — that is, from the chair of Moses.

SHEPHERDS AND HIRELINGS

I Seek Only Your Salvation

The hirelings take flight when they see a wolf or a robber. But, as I told you, from their superior position they can only command you to do good, not to swear falsely, and not to cheat or oppress anyone. But sometimes the way they live is such that they come to the bishop, seeking his advice on how to rob someone of a countryhouse. That has sometimes happened to me. I speak from experience, for I would not have believed it. Many seek evil advice from me, advice on lying and cheating, thinking to please me. But in Christ's name — and may what I say please our Lord — no such people have tempted me or found what they wanted in me, for if he who has called me wishes it, I am a shepherd, not a hireling. But what does the Apostle say? *It means little to me to be judged by you, or by human judgment. Nor do I judge myself, for I am not conscious of being guilty in any way. Still this does not justify me. It is our Lord who must judge me* (1 Corinthians 4:3-4).

Therefore, my conscience is not good because you praise it. Why praise something you cannot see? Let him praise who sees; let him also correct, if he sees something there that offends his sight. Not even I can say that I am completely sound, but I beat my breast and pray God *to have mercy on me* (Luke 18:13), and keep me from sin. Yet I think, for I speak in his presence, that I seek nothing from you other than your salvation, and often I groan at the sins of my fellow Christians. I am outraged, and tortured in mind, and sometimes I reproach them — or, rather, I never refuse to reproach them. All who remember what I say are witnesses to how many times I have reproached our sinful brothers and sisters, and reproached them severely.

Responsibilities of a Shepherd

Now I discuss my own responsibility with you. In Christ's name you are God's people, members of Christ, undivided in unity. You are in communion with the members of the apostles; you share the memory of the holy martyrs, scattered throughout the world, and you have been entrusted to my care so that I have to give a good account of you. But you know all about my program. Lord, you know I have spoken, that I have not kept silent; you know the spirit in which I have spoken, that I shed tears to you as I spoke, but they refused to listen to me. I think my account is blameless. The Holy Spirit, speaking through the prophet Ezekiel, has made me safe. You know the reading about the watchman: *You, son of man, I have appointed watchman for the house of Israel; when you hear me say anything, you shall warn them for me. If I tell the wicked that they shall surely die, and you do not speak out to dissuade the wicked from their ways,* [that is, I mean you to proclaim my words, and if you fail to do so *and the sword comes and carries them off,*] the wicked shall die for their guilt, but I will hold you responsible for their death. Why? Because he said nothing.

If the watchman sees the sword coming, and the trumpet sounds to warn them to flee, but they refuse to take any notice — that is, to correct themselves, to avoid the punishment which God threatens — *and the sword comes and carries some of them off, the wicked indeed die in their wickedness, but you save yourself* (Ezekiel 33:7-9). Also, in another well-known gospel passage, does he say anything different to the servant? The servant told him: *Sir, I know you are a hard and difficult man, for you reap where you have not sown, and gather up where you have not scattered, and so I went away in fear and hid your money in the ground. Here it is, take what belongs to you.* And he answered: *You lazy, good-for-nothing servant!* Because *you knew I was hard and difficult, reaping where I had not sown, and gathering where I had not scattered,* that very avarice of mine ought rather to have taught you that I expect a profit on my money. *Therefore, you ought to have given my money to the moneychangers so that when I returned I could have demanded my original sum with interest* (Luke 19:20-23). Did he not speak of giving and demanding? It is we, then, my friends, who give, but he will come to demand. Pray that he may find us ready.

CHAPTER 10

INTRODUCTION   *The gospel passage illustrated in the previous sermon (John 10:1-16) gives Augustine the occasion to show how Christ is the only true shepherd. The good shepherds who work in the Church are united with him as members of the head. Unity and love are the countersigns of the true shepherd. Only the first section of this sermon is given here, for the second section pertains to another theme.*

Sermon 138

UNITY THROUGH LOVE

The Good Shepherd and the Good Shepherds

*W*e have heard our Lord Jesus commending the office of the good shepherd to us. In that commendation, as we are given to understand, he has certainly warned us to be good shepherds ourselves. And yet to prevent us from thinking wrongly of a great number of shepherds, he says, *I am the good shepherd.* And he goes on to tell us why he is the good shepherd: *The good shepherd lays down his life for the sheep. But a hireling, and one who is not the shepherd, sees the wolf coming and takes to flight, because he does not care about the sheep, for he is a hireling* (John 10:11-12).

Therefore, Christ is the good shepherd. But what about Peter? Was he not a good shepherd? Did he not also lay down his life for the sheep? What about Paul? What about the rest of the apostles? What about the blessed martyr bishops of later times than theirs? What about our own holy Cyprian too? Were they not all good shepherds, and not hirelings of whom it is said, *Truly I tell you, they have received their reward* (Matthew 6:2)? All these were good shepherds, not only because they shed their blood, but because they did so for the sheep; it was not in pride that they shed their blood, but in love.

The Primacy of Love

For even among heretics, those who have suffered any vexations on account of their wickedness and errors, glory in the name of martyr, to cloak them in purity and so make it easier for them to steal, for they are the wolves. But if you want to know what to think of them, listen to a good shepherd, the apostle Paul, for you are not to presume that all who give up their bodies to death, even by fire, have shed their blood for the sheep, but some rather against the sheep. *If I speak,* he says, *in a human tongue or the tongue of angels, but have not love, I am like an echoing gong or jingling cymbal. If I know all mysteries and possess all prophecy and all faith, so that I can move mountains, but have not love, I am nothing* (1 Corinthians 13:1ff). Lastly, then, the faith that moves mountains is no mean possession. The things he mentions are indeed great, but if I have them without love, he says, it is not they but I who am nothing.

But so far he has not mentioned those who glory in a death they wrongly call martyrdom. Listen to how he refers to them, or rather transfixes them. *If I distribute all my goods to the poor, and give my body to the flames* (that indeed is their situation; but see what follows) *but have no love, it is no use to me* (1 Corinthians 13:3). So one may go to death, even to the shedding of one's blood or the burning of one's body, yet all to no avail because of the absence of love. Add love, and all is of use. Take away love, and the rest is no use.

Love, the Cement of Unity

How can we describe the goodness of that love, my friends? What is more precious, more full of light, stronger, more useful, and safer? God's gifts are many, and yet even bad people possess them, such as those who will say, *Lord, in your name we have prophesied, in your name we have cast out demons, and in your name we have performed many miracles.* He will not contradict them, for they would not dare lie in the presence of such a judge, or boast of things they had not done. But because they had no love, he will answer them all, *I do not know you* (Matthew 7:21-23).

But how can those who do not even love the unity of people living together have even a little love? In commending this unity to good shepherds, our Lord refused to refer to many shepherds. As I have already said, it is not that Peter was not a good shepherd, or Paul, or the rest of the apostles, or the later holy bishops, or blessed Cyprian. All these were good shepherds, and yet it was not good shepherds in general that he commended to good shepherds, but the one good shepherd. *I*, he said, *am the good shepherd* (John 10:11).

A Good Shepherd: Peter

Let us question our Lord as intelligently as we can, and enter into discussion with the utmost humility, since we are speaking with so great a head of so great a household. What do you mean, Lord, you who are the good shepherd? It is you, the good Lamb, who tells us that you are the good shepherd; you are the shepherd and the pastures, the lamb and the lion. What do you mean?

We must listen, and you must help us understand. *I, you say, am the good shepherd.* What was Peter? Was he not a shepherd, or was he a bad one? Let us see if he was not a shepherd. *Do you love me?* That was what you asked him, Lord: *Do you love me?* He answered, *Yes, I love you.* And so you told him, *Feed my sheep* (John 21:15-17). You, Lord, by your question, and by the confirmation of your own words, made the one who loved you a shepherd. Therefore, he, to whom you entrusted the feeding of your sheep, is a shepherd. He is a shepherd at your own recommendation. Now let us see whether or not he is good. We can find out from that very question and his own answer. You asked him whether he loved you, and he answered, *Yes, I love you.*

You saw into his heart, and saw that his answer was true. Is he not good, then, for loving someone so good? Why did he give that answer from the depths of his heart? Why was Peter saddened by the fact that, though you could see into his heart, you asked him not only once but again and yet a third time, so that the triple confession of love might blot out the triple sin of denial? Why, then, was he saddened by the repeated questioning of one who knew what he was asking, and had given what he heard? Why, though saddened, did he answer in these words: *Lord, you know all things; you yourself know that I love you*? Could one who made such a confession, uttered from the depths of his heart, really tell a lie? So, in saying that he loved you, and speaking from his inmost heart, he answered truthfully. Moreover, you have told us, *Good people speak good words from the good treasure house of their hearts* (Matthew 12:35). Therefore he was a shepherd, and a good shepherd — nothing, indeed, compared to the power and goodness of the shepherd of shepherds, yet even he was a shepherd, and was also good. And in the same way the rest were good shepherds.

The One Shepherd, Center of Christian Unity

What do you intend, then, in commending one shepherd to good shepherds, if not to teach unity in the figure of one shepherd? Our Lord himself explains it more clearly through our ministry, reminding you from the very gospel, and saying, Listen to what I have commended, *I am the good shepherd,* by which I meant: that all the rest, all good shepherds, are my members. There is one head, one body, one Christ. Therefore there is the

UNITY THROUGH LOVE

shepherd of shepherds, the shepherds who belong under one shepherd, and the sheep with their shepherds under one shepherd. Is this not what the Apostle says: *For just as the body is one and has many members, but though its members are many, they are all one body. The same is true of Christ* (1 Corinthians 2:12)? If the same is true of Christ, then since Christ includes all good shepherds within himself, he rightly commends one, saying, *I am the good shepherd.* I am, in other words I am one, and in unity with me all are one. He who feeds his sheep outside me feeds them against me. *He who does not gather them with me scatters them* (Matthew 12:30).

Listen to this unity more strongly commended: *I have other sheep,* he says, *who are not of this fold* (John 10:16). He was speaking to the first fold, those who were Jews by birth. But there were others who were Jews by faith as well, and still outside the fold among the Gentiles, those who were predestined, but not yet gathered into the fold. He knew those he had predestined; he knew those he had come to redeem by the shedding of his blood. He knew those who were destined to believe in him, though they had not yet seen him; he knew them, though they did not yet believe in him. *I have other sheep,* he says, *who are not of this fold,* for they are not Jews by birth. Yet they will not be outside this fold, for *I must bring them in, to make one flock with one shepherd* (John 10:16).

Published with the aid of a grant from
Mr. and Mrs. Paul Henkels.

"We Are Your Servants"